THE HAZARDOUS EARTH

CLIMATE CHANGE

Shifting Glaciers, Deserts, and Climate Belts

THE HAZARDOUS EARTH

CLIMATE CHANGE

Shifting Glaciers, Deserts, and Climate Belts

Timothy Kusky, Ph.D.

Facts On File
An imprint of Infobase Publishing

CLIMATE CHANGE: Shifting Glaciers, Deserts, and Climate Belts

Facts On File, Inc.
An imprint of Infobase Publishing
132 West 31st Street
New York NY 10001

Library of Congress Cataloging-in-Publication Data

Kusky, Timothy M.
    Climate change : shifting glaciers, deserts, and climate belts / Timothy Kusky.
        p. cm.— (Hazardous Earth)
    Includes bibliographical references and index.
    ISBN-13: 978-0-8160-6466-3
    ISBN-10: 0-8160-6466-0
    1. Climatic changes. 2. Climatic changes—Environmental aspects.
    3. Climatic zones. I. Title.
    QC981.8.C5K876 2009
    551.6—dc22   2008005134

Facts On File books are available at special discounts when purchased in bulk quantities for businesses, associations, institutions, or sales promotions. Please call our Special Sales Department in New York at (212) 967-8800 or (800) 322-8755.

You can find Facts On File on the World Wide Web at http://www.factsonfile.com

Text design by Erika K. Arroyo
Illustrations by Richard Garratt
Photo research by Suzanne M. Tibor, Ph.D.

Printed in the United States of America

VB FOF 10 9 8 7 6 5 4 3 2 1

This book is printed on acid-free paper and contains 30 percent postconsumer recycled contents.

To the 100 million people who live
within three feet of present-day sea level

Contents

Preface

Natural geologic hazards arise from the interaction of natural Earth processes and humans. Recent natural disasters such as the 2004 Indian Ocean tsunami that killed more than a quarter million people and earthquakes in Iran, Turkey, and Japan have shown how the motion of Earth's tectonic plates can suddenly make apparently safe environments dangerous or even deadly. The slow sinking of the land surface along many seashores has made many of the world's coastal regions prone to damage by ocean storms, as shown disastrously by Hurricane Katrina in 2005. Other natural Earth hazards arise gradually, such as the migration of poisonous radon gas into people's homes. Knowledge of Earth's natural hazards can lead one to live a safer life, providing guiding principles on where to build homes, where to travel, and what to do during natural hazard emergencies.

The eight-volume The Hazardous Earth set is intended to provide middle- and high-school readers with an accessible yet comprehensive account of natural geologic hazards, the geologic processes that create the hazards to humans, and what can be done to minimize their effects. Titles in the set present clear descriptions of plate tectonics and associated hazards, including earthquakes, volcanic eruptions, landslides, and soil and mineral hazards, as well as hazards resulting from the interaction of the ocean, atmosphere, and land, such as tsunamis, hurricanes, floods, and drought. After providing the reader with an in-depth knowledge of naturally hazardous processes, each volume gives vivid accounts of historic disasters and events that have shaped human history and serve as examples for future generations.

One volume covers the basic principles of plate tectonics and earthquake hazards, and another volume covers hazards associated with volcanoes. A third volume is about tsunamis and related wave phenomena, and another volume covers landslides and soil and mineral hazards, including discussions of mass wasting processes, soils, and the dangers of the natural concentration of hazardous elements such as radon. A fifth volume covers hazards from climate change and drought changing the land surface and how they affect human populations. This volume also discusses glacial environments and landforms, shifting climates, and desertification, all related to the planet's oscillations back and forth into ice ages and hothouses. Greater understanding is achieved by discussing environments on Earth that resemble icehouse (glaciers) and hothouse (desert) conditions. A sixth volume, entitled *The Coast,* includes discussion of hazards associated with hurricanes, coastal subsidence, and the impact of building along coastlines. A seventh volume, *Floods,* discusses river flooding and flood disasters, as well as many of the contemporary issues associated with the world's diminishing freshwater supply in the face of a growing population. This book also includes a chapter on sinkholes and phenomena related to water overuse. An eighth volume, *Asteroids and Meteorites,* presents information on impacts that have affected Earth, their effects, and the chances that another impact may occur soon on Earth.

The Hazardous Earth set is intended overall to be a reference book set for middle school, high school, and undergraduate college students, teachers and professors, scientists, librarians, journalists, and anyone who may be looking for information about Earth processes that may be hazardous to humans. The set is well illustrated with photographs and other illustrations, including line art, graphs, and tables. Each volume stands alone and can also be used in sequence with other volumes of the set in a natural hazards or disasters curriculum.

Acknowledgments

Many people have helped me with different aspects of preparing this volume. I would especially like to thank Carolyn, my wife, and my children, Shoshana and Daniel, for their patience during the long hours spent at my desk preparing this book. Without their understanding this work would not have been possible. Frank Darmstadt, executive editor at Facts On File, reviewed and edited all text and figures, providing guidance and consistency throughout. The excellent photo research provided by Suzie Tibor is appreciated and she is responsible for locating many of the excellent photographs in this volume. Many sections of the work draw from my own experiences doing scientific research in different parts of the world, and it is not possible to thank the hundreds of colleagues whose collaborations and work I have related in this book. Their contributions to the science that allowed the writing of this volume are greatly appreciated. I have tried to reference the most relevant works, or in some cases more recent sources that have more extensive reference lists. Any omissions are unintentional.

Introduction

Earth has experienced many episodes of dramatic *climate change,* with different periods in Earth history seeing the planet much hotter or much colder than at present. There have been periods during which the entire planet has been covered in ice in a frozen, seemingly perpetual, winter; at other times Earth's surface has been scorchingly hot and dry; and at others, much of the planet has felt like a hot, wet sauna. Many scientists warn that the planet is currently becoming warmer at a rapid pace, and there will be significant consequences for the people and *ecosystems* on the planet.

There are many different variables that control *climate* and can change the planet rapidly from one condition to another. Most of these are related to variations in the amount of incoming solar *radiation* caused by astronomical variations in Earth's orbit. Other variables that can strongly influence long-term climate change are the amount of heat that is retained by the atmosphere and ocean and, on timescales of tens to hundreds of millions of years, the distribution of landmasses as they move about the planet from *plate tectonics.* Each of these changes operates with different time cycles, alternately causing the climate to become warmer and colder.

Very long-term climate changes include the gradual change of Earth's *atmosphere* from a global *hothouse* dominated by CO_2 and other *greenhouse gases* when Earth was young to an atmosphere rich in nitrogen and oxygen over the next couple of billion years. Fortunately, during

Harvesting beans at a bend in the Yellow River, where it emerges from the Tibetan Plateau near Shapotou, China. Across the river are sterile dunes that form the limit of the Gobi Desert, and on this side the fertile sediment where the agricultural valley begins. *(Corbis)*

the early history of Earth, the Sun was less luminous, and the planet was not exceedingly hot. Over time, the motion of the continents has alternately placed continents over the poles, which causes the continent to be covered in snow, reflecting more heat back to space and causing global cooling. Plate tectonics also has a complex interaction with concentrations of CO_2 in the atmosphere, for instance, by uplifting *carbonate* rocks to be exposed to the atmosphere during continental collisions. The $CaCO_3$ then combines with atmospheric CO_2, depositing it in the oceans. Thus, continental collisions and times of *supercontinent* formation are associated with drawdown and reduction of CO_2 from the atmosphere, global cooling, and sea level changes.

Orbital variations seem to be the main cause of climate variations on more observable geological time scales. The main time periods of these variations have alternations of hotter and colder times, varying with frequencies of 100,000, 41,000, 23,000, and 19,000 years. To understand the complexity of natural climate variations, the contributions from each of these main contributing factors must be added together to obtain a very complex curve of climate warming and cooling trends. Built on top of these long-term variations in climate are some shorter term variations that can change rapidly, caused by changes in ocean circulation, sunspot cycles, and finally, the contribution in the last couple of hundred years from the industry of people, called *anthropogenic* changes. Deciphering which of these variables is the cause of a particular percentage of the present global warming is no simple matter, and many political debates focus on whom to blame. Perhaps it is just as appropriate to be focusing on how the human race needs to respond to *global warming*. Coastal cities may need to be moved, crop belts are migrating, climate zones are changing, river conditions are going to be different, and many aspects of life that people are used to will be different. Considerable effort is being spent to understand the climate history of the past million years and to help predict the future.

In this book, different aspects of climate change are examined. First, the causes of climate change on these different time scales are examined in detail in the first few chapters, with the first chapter examining natural long-term climate changes and the evolution of the atmosphere and the second examining natural medium- to short-term causes of climate change. The third chapter assesses human-induced climate changes over the past couple of hundred years, and incorporates findings from the *Intergovernmental Panel on Climate Change* report "Climate Change 2007." Climate change is causing many of the *deserts* of the world to expand. Chapters 4 and 5 examine deserts and climate changes that lead to *drought* and *desertification*. The glacial ice caps, mountain *glaciers*, and *permafrost* regions of the world are shrinking under the influence

Fort Proctor, Mississippi Delta, Louisiana, surrounded by water due to regional subsidence of the delta and sea level rise *(Visuals Unlimited)*

Landforms of past glaciers including a moraine in the foreground *(Photo Researchers)*

of climate change. In chapter 6, glacial environments are described, and the past several million years of climate history of advancing and retreating *glacial periods* is analyzed. Chapter 7 examines how Earth has switched over its entire 4.5-billion-year history from one climate extreme to another and balances this history with the current climate changes that are likely to be induced by human injection of greenhouse gases into the atmosphere. Details of what the different changing climate zones and intervals may be like in the future are examined by looking in detail at past- and present-day desert and glacial climate zones on Earth. This chapter paints a picture of what the future Earth climate may be and what the human race needs to do to adapt to the rapidly changing climate. Much of chapter 8 follows the recommendations of the Intergovernmental Panel on Climate Change, which in late 2007 and 2008 issued a series of predictions and guidelines on how nations should be preparing for climate change in the coming century.

1

Natural Long-term Climate Change:
Atmospheric Evolution, Plate Tectonics, Supercontinents, and Solar Evolution

There are many controls that operate to change Earth's climate on different time scales. Some cause the global temperature to rise and fall with a time interval between warming and cooling influences of billions to hundreds of millions of years; others operate on millions to tens of millions of years time frames. These very slowly operating forces include the very slow evolution of the composition of the planet's atmosphere from an early greenhouse atmosphere when Earth had recently formed to its present day composition. During the earliest history of the solar system, the Sun was about 30 percent less luminous, so the temperature on Earth's surface was not as high as it would have been had those atmospheric conditions been extant when the atmosphere had its present composition. Changes in solar luminosity have been significant in Earth history and will be significant again in the future.

Plate tectonics exhibits controls of different types and with different time scales of influence on changing the atmospheric composition and climate. One type of influence of plate tectonics is that on a planetary scale, plate tectonics goes through intervals of time in which *sea-floor spreading* and volcanism is very active, and periods where it is less active. During the active times, the volcanism releases a lot of carbon dioxide and other greenhouse gases to the atmosphere, causing global warming. During inactive times, global cooling can result. These changes operate on time scales of tens to hundreds of millions of years. Periods of very active seafloor spreading are often associated with periods of breakup of large continental landmasses known as supercontinents, and thus breakup of continents is often associated with global warming. Periods of less active seafloor spreading are often associated with continental amalgamations, formation of supercontinents, and global cooling.

When continents collide, this process uplifts large sections of carbonate rocks from *passive margins* and exposes them to atmospheric weathering. When the calcium carbonate ($CaCO_3$) in these rocks is broken down by *chemical weathering,* the CO_3 ion is dissolved by rainwater, and the free Ca ion then combines with atmospheric CO_2 to form new layers of *limestone* in the ocean, drawing CO_2 down out of the atmosphere and causing global cooling.

The interaction between these different long-term drivers of global climate is thought to be largely responsible for the long-term fluctuations in global climate on the billions to hundreds to tens of millions of years time scales. Geologists and paleoclimatologists do not yet understand many aspects of these changes, but the mechanisms seem

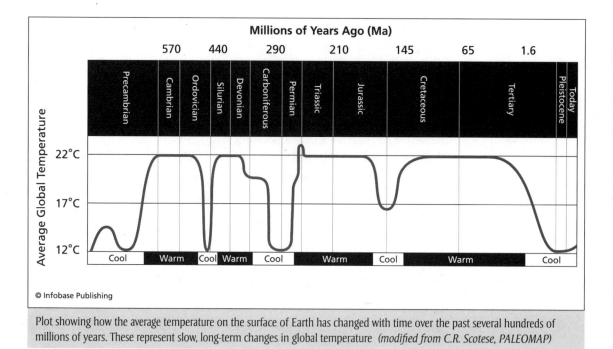

© Infobase Publishing

Plot showing how the average temperature on the surface of Earth has changed with time over the past several hundreds of millions of years. These represent slow, long-term changes in global temperature *(modified from C.R. Scotese, PALEOMAP)*

fairly well understood, and represent the most likely explanation for the causes of the changes.

In this chapter, the structure and evolution of the atmosphere is discussed, and then the long-term plate tectonic influences on climate are discussed.

Structure of the Atmosphere

The atmosphere is comprised of a sphere around Earth consisting of a mixture of gases, held in place by gravity. The most abundant gas is nitrogen (78 percent), followed by oxygen (21 percent), argon (0.9 percent), carbon dioxide (0.036 percent), and minor amounts of helium, krypton, neon, and xenon. Air pressure, or *atmospheric pressure*, is the force per unit area (similar to weight) that the air above a certain point exerts on any object below it. Atmospheric pressure causes most of the volume of the atmosphere to be compressed to 3.4 miles (5.5 km) above Earth's surface, even though the entire atmosphere is hundreds of kilometers thick. The atmosphere is divided into several layers, based mainly on the vertical temperature gradients that vary significantly with height. Atmospheric pressure and air density both decrease more uniformly with height, and therefore do not serve as a useful way to differentiate between different atmospheric layers. The lower 36,000 feet (10,972.8 m) of the atmosphere is known as the *troposphere*, where the temperature generally decreases gradually, at about 70°F per mile (6.4°C per km) with increasing height above the surface. This is because the Sun heats the surface that in turn warms the lower part of the troposphere.

Above the troposphere is a boundary region known as the tropopause, marking the transition into the *stratosphere*, which continues to a height of about 31 miles (50 km). The base of the stratosphere contains a region known as an isothermal, where the temperature remains the same with increasing height. The tropopause is generally at higher elevations in the summer than the winter and is also the region where the jet streams are located. Jet streams are narrow, stream-like channels of air that flow at high velocities, often exceeding 115 miles per hour (100 knots). Above about 12.5 miles (20 km), the isothermal region gives way to the upper stratosphere where temperatures increase with height, back to near-surface temperatures at 31 miles (50 km). The heating of the stratosphere at this level is due to ozone absorbing ultraviolet radiation from the Sun.

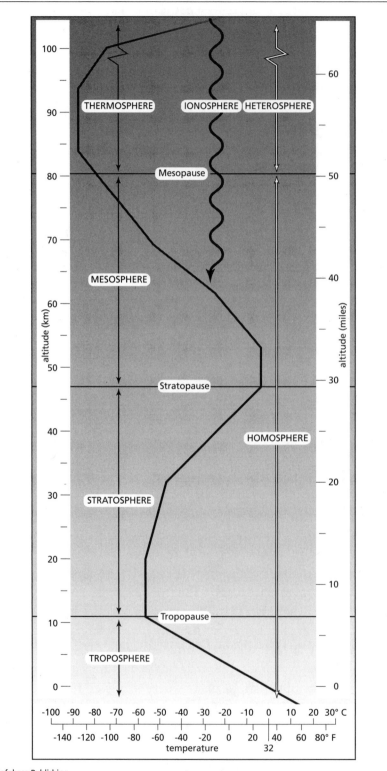

Opposite: Structure of the atmosphere, showing different layers and temperature profile

The *mesosphere* lies above the stratosphere, extending between 31 and 53 miles (50–85 km). An isothermal region known as the stratopause separates the stratosphere and mesosphere. The air temperature in the mesosphere decreases dramatically above the stratopause, reaching a low of –130°F (–90°C) at the top of the mesosphere. The mesopause separates the mesosphere from the thermosphere, which is a hot layer where temperatures rise to more than 150°F (80°C). The relatively few oxygen atoms at this level absorb solar energy and heat quickly and may change dramatically in response to changing solar activity. The *thermosphere* continues to thin upward, extending to about 311 miles (500 km) above the surface. Above this level, atoms dissociate and are able to shoot outward and escape the gravitational pull of Earth. This far region of the atmosphere is sometimes referred to as the exosphere.

In addition to the temperature-based division of the atmosphere, it is possible to divide the atmosphere into different regions based on their chemical and other properties. Using such a scheme, the lower 46.5–62 miles (75–100 km) of the atmosphere may be referred to as the homosphere, where the atmosphere is well mixed and has a fairly uniform ratio of gases from base to top. In the overlying heterosphere, the denser gases (oxygen, nitrogen) have settled to the base, whereas lighter gases (hydrogen, helium) have risen to greater heights, resulting in chemical differences with height.

The upper parts of the homosphere and the heterosphere contain a large number of electrically charged particles known as ions. This region is known also as the ionosphere, which strongly influences radio transmission and the formation of the *aurora* borealis and aurora australis.

Atmospheric gases are being produced at approximately the same rate that they are being destroyed or removed from the atmospheric system, although some gases are gradually increasing or decreasing in abundance as described below. Soil bacteria and other biologic agents remove nitrogen from the atmosphere, whereas decay of organic material releases nitrogen back to the atmosphere. However, decaying organic material removes oxygen from the atmosphere by combining it with other substances to produce oxides. Animals also remove oxygen from the atmosphere by breathing, whereas oxygen is added back to the atmosphere through *photosynthesis.*

Water vapor is an extremely important gas in the atmosphere, but it varies greatly in concentration (0–4 percent) from place to place and from time to time. Water vapor is invisible; atmospheric water only becomes visible as clouds, fog, ice, and rain when the water molecules coalesce into larger groups. Water forms as gas, liquid, or solid and constitutes the precipitation that falls to Earth and is the basis for the hydrologic cycle. Water vapor is also a major factor in heat transfer in the atmosphere. A kind of heat known as latent heat is released when water vapor turns into solid ice or liquid water. This heat is a major source of atmospheric energy that is a major contributor to the formation of thunderstorms, *hurricanes,* and other weather phenomena. Water vapor may also play a longer-term role in atmospheric regulation, as it is a greenhouse gas that absorbs a significant portion of the outgoing radiation from Earth, causing the atmosphere to warm.

Carbon dioxide, although small in concentration, is another very important gas in Earth's atmosphere. Carbon dioxide is produced during decay of organic material, from volcanic outgassing, from cow, termite, and other animal emissions, from deforestation, and from the burning of fossil fuels. It is taken up by plants during photosynthesis and is also used by many marine organisms for their shells, made of $CaCO_3$ (calcium carbonate). When these organisms (for instance, phytoplankton) die, their shells can sink to the bottom of the ocean and be buried, removing carbon dioxide from the atmospheric system. Like water vapor, carbon dioxide is a greenhouse gas that traps some of the outgoing solar radiation that is reflected from Earth, causing the atmosphere to warm up. Because carbon dioxide is released by the burning of fossil fuels, its concentration is increasing in the atmosphere as humans consume more fuel. The concentration of CO_2 in the atmosphere has increased by 15 percent since 1958, enough to cause considerable global warming. It is estimated that the concentration of CO_2 will increase by another 35 percent by the end of the 21st century, further enhancing global warming. Other gases also contribute to the greenhouse effect, notably methane (CH_4), nitrous oxide (NO_2), and chlorofluorocarbons (CFC's). Methane is increasing in concentration in the atmosphere. It is produced by the breakdown of organic material by bacteria in rice paddies and other environments, termites, and in the stomachs of cows. NO_2, produced by microbes in the soil, is also increasing in concentration by 1 percent every few years, even though it is destroyed by ultraviolet radiation in the atmosphere. *Chlorofluorocarbons* have received a large amount of attention since they are long-lived greenhouse gases increasing in atmospheric concentration as a result of human activity. Chlorofluorocarbons trap heat like other greenhouse gases and also destroy ozone (O_3), the protective blanket that shields Earth from harmful ultraviolet radiation. Chlorofluorocarbons were used widely as refrigerants and as propellants in spray cans. Their use has been largely curtailed, but since they have such a long residence time in the atmosphere, they are still destroying ozone and contributing to global warming and will continue to do so for many years.

Ozone (O_3) is found primarily in the upper atmosphere where free oxygen atoms combine with oxygen molecules (O_2) in the stratosphere. The loss of ozone has been dramatic in recent years, even leading to the formation of "ozone holes" with virtually no ozone present above the Arctic and Antarctic in the fall. There is currently debate about how much of the ozone loss is due to human-induced ozone loss by chlorofluorocarbon production and how much may be related to natural fluctuations in ozone concentration.

Many other gases and particulate matter play important roles in atmospheric phenomena. For instance, small amounts of sulfur dioxide (SO_2) produced by the burning of fossil fuels mix with water to form sulfuric acid, the main harmful component of acid rain. *Acid rain* is killing the biota of many natural lake systems, particularly in the northeastern United States, and it is causing a wide range of other environmental problems across the world. Other pollutants are major causes of respiratory problems and environmental degradation, and the major increase in particulate matter in the atmosphere in the past century has increased the hazards and health effects from these atmospheric particles.

The atmosphere is always moving, because more of the Sun's heat is received per unit area at the equator than at the poles. The heated air expands and rises to where it spreads out, and then it cools and sinks and gradually returns to the equator. This pattern of global air circulation forms *Hadley Cells* that mix air between the equator and mid-latitudes. Hadley Cells are belts of air that encircle Earth, rising along the equator, dropping moisture as they rise in the tropics. As the air moves away from the equator at high elevations, it cools, becomes drier, and then descends at 15–30°N and S latitude where it either returns to the equator or moves toward the poles. The locations of the Hadley Cells move north and south annually in response to the changing apparent seasonal movement of the Sun. High-pressure systems form where the air descends, characterized by stable clear skies and intense evaporation,

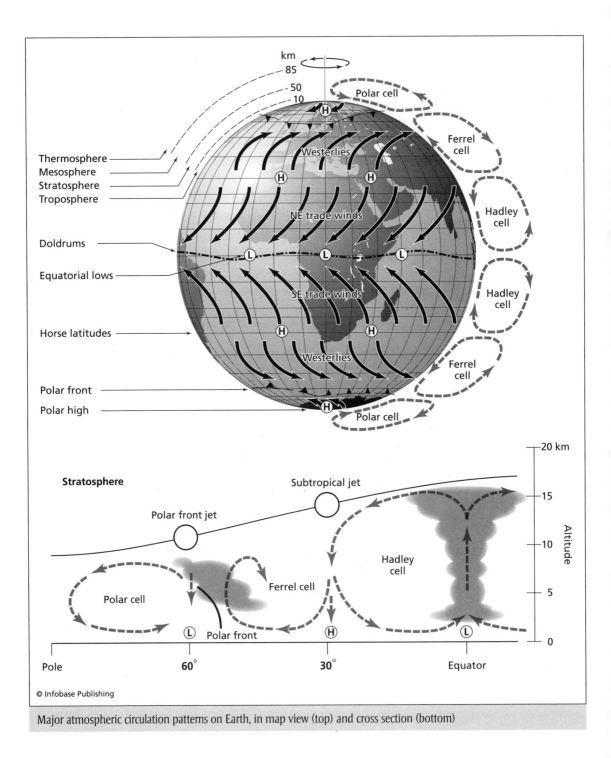

Major atmospheric circulation patterns on Earth, in map view (top) and cross section (bottom)

because the air is so dry. Another pair of major global circulation belts is formed as air cools at the poles and spreads toward the equator. Cold polar fronts form where the polar air mass meets the warmer air that has circulated around the Hadley Cell from the tropics. In the belts between the polar front and the Hadley Cells, strong westerly winds develop. The position of the polar front and extent of the west-moving wind is controlled by the position of the polar *jet stream* (formed in the upper troposphere), which is partly fixed in place in the Northern Hemisphere by the high Tibetan Plateau and the Rocky Mountains. Dips and bends in the jet stream path are known as *Rossby Waves*, and these partly determine the location of high- and low-pressure systems. These Rossby Waves tend to be semi-stable in different seasons and have predictable patterns for summer and winter. If the pattern of Rossby Waves in the jet stream changes significantly for a season or longer, it may cause storm systems to track to different locations than normal, causing local droughts or floods. Changes to this global circulation may also change the locations of regional downwelling, cold dry air. This can cause long-term drought and desertification. Such changes may persist for periods of several weeks, months, or years, and may explain several of the severe droughts that have affected Asia, Africa, North America, and elsewhere.

Circulation cells similar to Hadley Cells mix air in middle to high latitudes and between the poles and high latitudes. The effects of Earth's rotation modify this simple picture of the atmosphere's circulation. The *Coriolis effect* causes any freely moving body in the Northern Hemisphere to veer to the right, and in the Southern Hemisphere to the left. The combination of these effects forms the familiar trade winds, easterlies and westerlies, and doldrums.

Evolution of the Atmosphere

There is considerable uncertainty about the origin and composition of Earth's earliest atmosphere and the temperature and atmospheric pressure at the surface of Earth. Many models assume that methane and ammonia dominated the planet's early atmosphere instead of nitrogen and carbon dioxide, as at present. The gases that formed the early atmosphere could have come from volcanic outgassing by volcanoes, from extraterrestrial sources (principally cometary impacts), or, most likely, both. It is also likely that comets brought organic molecules to Earth. A very large late impact is thought to have melted outer parts of Earth, formed the Moon, and blown away the earliest atmosphere. The present atmosphere must therefore represent a later, secondary atmosphere formed after this late impact.

During the early *Archaean,* the Sun was only about 70 percent as luminous as it is presently, so Earth must have experienced a greenhouse warming effect to keep temperatures above the freezing point of water but below the boiling point. Increased levels of carbon dioxide and ammonia in the early atmosphere could have acted as greenhouse gases, accounting for the remarkable maintenance of global temperatures within the stability field of liquid water, allowing the development of life. Much of the carbon dioxide that was in the early atmosphere is now locked up in deposits of sedimentary limestone and in the planet's biomass. The carbon dioxide that shielded the early Earth and kept temperatures in the range suitable for life to evolve now forms the bodies and remains of those very life forms.

Role of the Atmosphere in Climate Change

Interactions between the atmosphere, *hydrosphere, biosphere,* and *lithosphere* control global climate. Global climate represents a balance between the amount of solar radiation received and the amount of this energy that is retained in a given area. The planet receives about 2.4 times as much heat in the equatorial regions compared to the polar regions. The atmosphere and oceans respond to this unequal heating by setting up currents and circulation systems that redistribute the heat more equally. These circulation patterns are in turn affected by the ever-changing pattern of the distribution of continents, oceans, and mountain ranges.

The amounts and types of gases in the atmosphere can modify the amount of incoming solar radiation, and hence global temperature. For instance, cloud cover can cause much of the incoming solar radiation to be reflected back to space before being trapped by the lower atmosphere. On the other hand, greenhouse gases allow incoming short wavelength solar radiation to enter the atmosphere, but trap this radiation when it tries to escape in its longer wavelength reflected form. This causes a buildup of heat in the atmosphere and can lead to a global warming known as the greenhouse effect.

The amount of heat trapped in the atmosphere by greenhouse gases has varied greatly over Earth's history. One of the most important greenhouse gases is carbon dioxide (CO_2). Plants, which release O_2 to the atmosphere, now take up CO_2 by photosynthesis. In the early part of Earth's history (in the *Precambrian,* before plants covered the land surface), photosynthesis did not remove CO_2 from the atmosphere, with the result that CO_2 levels were much higher than at present. Atmospheric CO_2 is also presently taken up by marine organisms that remove it from the ocean surface water (which is in equilibrium with the atmosphere); they use the CO_2 along with calcium to form their shells and mineralized tissue. These organisms make $CaCO_3$ (calcite), which is the main component of limestone, a rock composed largely of the dead remains of marine organisms. Approximately 99 percent of the

WHEN WILL THE SUN EXPAND TO MAKE EARTH UNINHABITABLE?

Stars like the Sun at the center of Earth's solar system undergo a series of evolutionary stages, characterized by burning of different fuels such as hydrogen and helium, different luminosity and output of radiation, and different radii from the star's center. Stars with a mass approximately equal to the Sun follow a sequence known as the main sequence, where they burn hydrogen and do not change for about 90 percent of their history. However, when the hydrogen fuel begins to run out, the star can deviate off the main sequence of evolution and meet drastically different ends depending primarily on its mass. Most models for Earth's Sun predict that it will eventually expand by several hundred times its present diameter to become a red supergiant that will grow so large that it will encompass the inner planets of the solar system, including Earth. This happens as a reaction of the outer layers of the star to the contraction of the center of the star as its hydrogen fuel is expended and typically happens in two stages. The first expansion, known as the Red Giant Branch or RGB phase of stellar evolution, ends with the ignition of helium burning in the star's core, and the second expansion (the Asymptotic Giant Branch or AGB stage of stellar evolution) occurs when the core has consumed all of its helium. Earth's Sun is expected to expand into a red supergiant with a radius that extends beyond Earth in about 7.5 billion years. That will be the most significant global warming event the planet will ever see. However, before that stage the Sun will go through another less dramatic stage that will double the solar luminosity and mean the end for a habitable world on planet Earth. Luckily, this other event is not due until about 2 billion years before the ultimate cooking of Earth, in about 5.5 billion years from now. Some models predict that during stellar evolution the Sun will lose more mass than the classical models predict, and that the radius of the Sun will not quite reach Earth (but will reach Venus). The result will be the same—present-day global warming will seem insignificant, and the planet will be uninhabitable by any known life forms. Calculations can be made about when the solar expansion will make Earth uninhabitable everywhere, and the human race will have to seek a place farther in the solar system or in interstellar space to survive. If the solar expansion alone were to heat the current Earth it would take about 800 million years to raise the temperature to what is predicted to be reached by 2100 or 2150, meaning that human emission of greenhouse gases is accelerating the solar luminosity effect by 10 million times. Models suggest that when the average temperature of Earth reaches 140°F (60°C) the planet will be uninhabitable by humans. The conservative models for solar evolution suggest that this point will be crossed in another 5.7 billion years, a comfortable time margin for the human race to seek technology to find a new home.

planet's CO_2 is presently removed from the atmosphere/ocean system because it is locked up in rock deposits of limestone on the continents and on the sea floor. If this amount of CO_2 were released back into the atmosphere, the global temperature would increase dramatically. In the early Precambrian when this CO_2 was free in the atmosphere, global temperatures averaged about 550°F (290°C).

The atmosphere redistributes heat quickly by forming and redistributing clouds and uncondensed water vapor around the planet along atmospheric circulation cells. Oceans are able to hold and redistribute more heat because of the greater amount of water in the oceans, but they redistribute this heat more slowly than the atmosphere. Surface currents are formed in response to wind patterns, but deep ocean currents that move more of the planet's heat follow courses that are more related to the bathymetry (topography of the seafloor) and the spinning of Earth than they are related to surface winds.

The balance of incoming and outgoing heat from Earth has determined the overall temperature of the planet through time. Examination of the geological record has enabled paleoclimatologists to reconstruct periods when Earth had glacial periods, hot dry periods, hot wet periods, or cold dry periods. In most cases, Earth has responded to these changes by expanding and contracting its climate belts. Warm periods see an expansion of the warm subtropical belts to high latitudes, and cold periods see an expansion of the cold climates of the poles to low latitudes.

Plate Tectonics and Climate

The outer layers of Earth are broken into about a dozen large tectonic plates, extending to about 60–100 miles (100–160 km) beneath the surface. Each of these plates may be made of oceanic crust and lithosphere, of continental crust and lithosphere, or of an oceanic plate with a continent occupying part of the area of the plate. Plate tectonics describes processes associated with the movement of these plates along three different types of boundaries, divergent, convergent, and *transform*. At *divergent boundaries* the plates move apart from one another, and molten rock (*magma*) rises from the mantle to fill the space between the diverging plates. This magma makes long ridges of volcanoes along a *mid-ocean ridge system* that accounts for most of the volcanism on the planet. These volcanoes emit huge quantities of carbon dioxide (CO_2) and other gases while they erupt. There have been times in the history of Earth that mid-ocean ridge volcanism was very active, producing huge quantities of magma and CO_2 gas, and other times when the volcanism is relatively inactive. The large quantities of magma and volcanism involved in this process have ensured that variations in mid-ocean ridge magma production have exerted strong controls on the amount of CO_2 in the atmosphere and ocean, and thus, are closely linked with climate. Periods of voluminous magma production are correlated with times of high atmospheric CO_2 and global warm periods. These times are also associated with times of high sea levels, since the extra volcanic and hot oceanic material on the sea floor takes up extra volume and displaces the seawater to rise higher over the continents. This rise in sea levels in turn buried many rocks that are then taken out of the chemical weathering system, slowing down reactions between the atmosphere and the weathering of rocks. Those reactions are responsible for removing large quantities of CO_2 from the atmosphere, so the rise in sea level serves to further promote global warming during periods of active seafloor volcanism.

Convergent boundaries are places where two plates are moving toward each other, or colliding. Most plate convergence happens where an oceanic plate is pushed or subducted beneath another plate, either oceanic or continental, forming a line of volcanoes on the overriding plate. This line of volcanoes is known as a magmatic arc, and specifically as an island arc if built on oceanic crust, and an Andean arc if built on continental crust. When continents on these plates collide, the rocks that were deposited along their margins, typically underwater, are uplifted in the collision zone and exposed to weathering processes. The weathering of these rocks, particularly the limestone and carbonate rocks, causes chemical reactions where the CO_2 in the atmosphere reacts with the products of weathering and forms new carbonate ($CaCO_3$) that gets deposited in the oceans. Continental collisions are thus associated with the overall removal of CO_2 from the atmosphere and help promote global cooling.

Transform margins do not significantly influence global climate, since they are not associated with large amounts of volcanism, nor do they uplift large quantities of rock from the ocean.

The time scale of variations in global CO_2 related to changes in plate tectonics are slow and fall under the realm of causing very long-term climate changes, in millions to tens of millions of years long cycles. Plate tectonics and movement of continents has been associated with glaciations for the past few billion years, but the exact link between tectonics and climate is not clearly established. Some doubt remains as to why global temperatures dropped inducing the various glacial ages. The answer may be related to changes in the natural (non-biogenic) production rate of carbon dioxide—the number one greenhouse gas. CO_2 is produced in volcanoes and in the mid-ocean ridges. It is lost by being slowly absorbed in the oceans. Both of these processes are very slow—about the right time scales to explain the *Great Ice Ages.* One theory is that carbon dioxide is produced by a faster rate of seafloor spreading and a subsequent increase in volcanism. During times of rapid spreading, the higher volcanic activity, coupled with higher sea levels and reduced chemical weathering of rocks, may promote global warming by enriching the CO_2 content of the atmosphere. Similarly, global cooling may result from stalled or slowed spreading.

Supercontinents and Climate

The motion of the tectonic plates periodically causes most of the continental land masses of the planet to collide with each other, forming giant continents known as supercontinents. For much of the past several billion years, these supercontinents have alternately formed and broken up, in a process called the supercontinent cycle. The last supercontinent was known as *Pangaea,* which broke up about 160 million years ago to form the present day plates on the planet. Before that the previous supercontinent was known as *Gondwana,* which formed about 600–500 million years ago, and the one before that was known as Rodinia, formed around a billion years ago.

The distribution of land masses and formation and breakup of supercontinents has dramatically influenced global and local climate on time scales of 100 million years, with cycles repeating for the past few billion years of Earth history. The supercontinent cycle predicts that the planet should have periods of global warming associated with supercontinent breakup and global cooling associated with supercontinent formation. The supercontinent cycle affects sea level changes, initiates periods of global glaciation, changes the global climate from hothouse to icehouse conditions, and influences seawater salinity and nutrient supply. All of these consequences of plate tectonics have profound influences on life on Earth.

Sea level has changed by thousands of feet (hundreds of meters) above and below current levels at many times in Earth history. In fact, sea level is constantly changing in response to a number of different variables, many of them related to plate tectonics, the supercontinent cycle, and climate. Sea level was 1,970 feet (600 m) higher than now during the Ordovician and reached a low stand at the end of the Permian. Sea levels were high again in the Cretaceous during the breakup of the supercontinent of Pangaea.

Sea levels may change at different rates and amounts in response to different phases of the supercontinent cycle, and the sea level changes are closely related to climate. The global volume of the mid-ocean ridges can change dramatically, either by increasing the total length of ridges or changing the rate of seafloor spreading. Either process produces more volcanism, increases the volume of volcanoes on the seafloor raising sea levels, and puts a lot of extra CO_2 into the atmosphere, raising global temperatures. The total length of ridges typically increases during continental breakup, since continents are being rifted apart and some continental rifts can evolve into mid-ocean ridges. Additionally, if seafloor spreading rates are increased, the amount of young, topographically elevated ridges is increased relative to the slower, older topographically lower ridges that occupy a smaller volume. If the volume of the ridges increases by either mechanism, then a volume of water equal to the increased ridge volume is displaced and *sea level rises,* inundating the continents. Changes in ridge volume are able to change sea levels positively or negatively by about 985 feet (300 m) from present values, at rates of about 0.4 inch (1 cm) every 1,000 years.

Continent-continent collisions, such as those associated with supercontinent formation, can lower sea levels by reducing the area of the continents. When continents collide, mountains and plateaus are uplifted, and the amount of material that is taken from below sea level to higher elevations no longer displaces seawater, causing sea levels to drop. The contemporaneous India-Asia collision has caused sea levels to drop by 33 feet (10 m). Times when supercontinents amalgamate are associated with times when sea level drops to low levels.

Other things, such as mid-plate volcanism, can also change sea levels. The Hawaiian Islands are hot-spot style mid-plate volcanoes that have been erupted onto the seafloor, displacing an amount of water equal to their volume. Although this effect is not large at present, at some periods in Earth history there were many more *hot spots* (such as in the Cretaceous), and the effect may have been larger.

The effects of the supercontinent cycle on sea level may be summarized as follows. Continent assembly favors *regression,* whereas continental fragmentation and dispersal favors *transgression.* Regressions

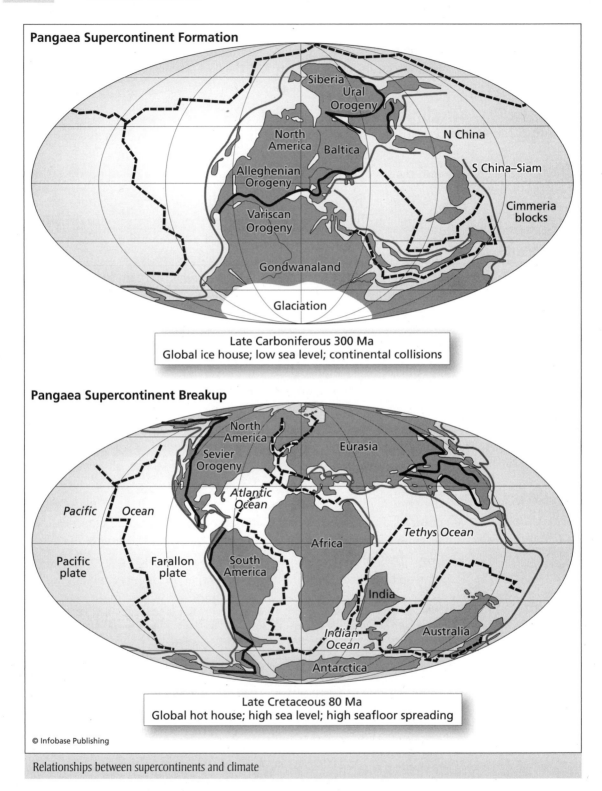

Pangaea Supercontinent Formation

Siberia
Ural Orogeny
North America
Baltica
N China
Alleghenian Orogeny
S China–Siam
Cimmeria blocks
Variscan Orogeny
Gondwanaland
Glaciation

Late Carboniferous 300 Ma
Global ice house; low sea level; continental collisions

Pangaea Supercontinent Breakup

North America
Sevier Orogeny
Eurasia
Atlantic Ocean
Pacific   Ocean
Tethys Ocean
Pacific plate
Farallon plate
Africa
South America
India
Indian Ocean
Australia
Antarctica

Late Cretaceous 80 Ma
Global hot house; high sea level; high seafloor spreading

© Infobase Publishing

Relationships between supercontinents and climate

followed formation of the supercontinents of Rodinia and Pangaea, whereas transgressions followed the fragmentation of Rodinia and the Jurassic-Cretaceous breakup of Pangaea.

Climate and Seasonality

Variations in the average weather at different times of the year are known as *seasons*, controlled by the average amount of solar radiation received at the surface in a specific place for a certain time period. The amount of radiation received at a particular point on the surface is determined by several things, including the angle at which the Sun's rays hit the surface, the length of time the rays warm the surface, and the distance to the Sun. As Earth orbits the Sun approximately once every 365 days, it follows an elliptical orbit that brings it closest to the Sun in January (91 million miles [147 million km]) and farthest from the Sun in July (94.5 million miles [152 million km]). Therefore, the Sun's rays are slightly more intense in January than in July but, as any Northern Hemisphere resident can testify, this must not be the main controlling factor on determining seasonal warmth, since winters in the Northern Hemisphere are colder than summers. Where the Sun's rays hit a surface directly, at right angles to the surface, they are most effective at warming the surface, since they are not being spread out over a larger area on an inclined surface. Also, where the Sun's rays enter the atmosphere directly they travel through the least amount of atmosphere, so are weakened much less than rays that must travel obliquely through the atmosphere, which absorbs some of their energy.

Earth's rotational axis is presently inclined at 23.5° from perpendicular to the plane it rotates on around the Sun (the ecliptic plane), causing different hemispheres of the planet to be tilted toward or away from the Sun in different seasons. In the Northern Hemisphere summer, the Northern Hemisphere is tilted toward the Sun, so it receives more direct sunlight rays than the Southern Hemisphere, causing more heating in the north than in the south. Also, it receives direct sunlight for longer periods of time than the Southern Hemisphere, enhancing this effect. On the summer solstice on June 21, the Sun's rays are directly hitting 23.5°N latitude (called the tropic of Cancer) at noon. Because of the tilt of the planet, the Sun does not set below the horizon for all points north of the Arctic Circle (66.5°N). Points farther south have progressively shorter days, and points farther north have progressively longer days. At the North Pole, the Sun rises above the horizon on March 20th and does not set again until six months later on September 22.

However, since the Sun's rays are so oblique in these northern latitudes, they receive less solar radiation than areas farther south where the rays hit more directly, but for shorter times. As Earth rotates around the Sun, it finds the Southern Hemisphere tilted at its maximum amount toward the Sun on December 21, and the situation is reversed from the Northern Hemisphere summer, so that the same effects occur in the southern latitudes.

Seasonal variations in temperature and rainfall at specific places are complicated by global atmospheric circulation cells, proximity to large bodies of water and warm or cold ocean currents, and monsoon type effects in some parts of the world. Some seasons in some places are hot and wet, others are hot and dry, cold and wet, or cold and dry.

Supercontinents affect the supply of nutrients to the oceans, and thus, seasonality. Large supercontinents cause increased seasonality, and thus lead to an increase in the nutrient supply through overturning of the ocean waters. During breakup and dispersal, smaller continents have less seasonality, yielding decreased vertical mixing, leaving fewer nutrients in shelf waters. Seafloor spreading also increases the nutrient supply to the ocean; the more active the seafloor spreading system, the more interaction there is between ocean waters and crustal minerals that get dissolved to form nutrients in the seawater.

Conclusion

Earth's climate is always changing, under the influence of a number of different factors that operate over different time scales. This chapter has examined the structure of the atmosphere and the long- to medium-term effects that can change global climate. The long-term evolution of the atmosphere has changed from an early global greenhouse in which the planet had huge amounts of carbon dioxide. At this time the Sun was less luminous, so the overall temperature on the surface was not much greater than today. Over time, the carbon dioxide was gradually buried in rocks, and plants began increasing the oxygen content of the atmosphere until the present levels were reached. Global atmospheric and oceanic circulation patterns redistribute heat on the planet, moving it from equatorial regions that receive more solar energy than polar regions.

Climate can change on very long, slow time scales from changes in the amount of carbon dioxide and other greenhouse gases that are vented from volcanic systems on Earth. Most of the world's volcanoes are located along the mid-ocean ridge system, so changes in the amount or rate of volcanism and spreading along the ridges can dramatically change the amount of carbon dioxide in the atmosphere. Global warming is generally associated with increased amounts of seafloor spreading when large masses of continents, called supercontinents, break apart. The increased amount of volcanism also displaces large amounts of water, leading to sea level rise during continental breakup. Conversely, when many continental blocks converge and collide, the carbonate and silicate minerals buried in rocks along the continental margins get exposed to weathering and combine with atmospheric carbon dioxide, causing global cooling. The uplift of rocks out of the ocean during collisions, plus the global cooling, often leads to major glaciations and icehouse conditions for the planet during major continental collisions.

2

Natural Medium-
and Short-term
Climate Change

Astronomical Forcing, El Niño–
Southern Oscillation, Thermohaline
Circulation, and Massive Volcanism

Plate tectonics, supercontinents, and massive volcanism can cause climate variations on time scales of millions to billions of years. Many other variables contribute to climate variations that operate on shorter-term time scales, many of which are more observable to people. Variations in Earth's orbit around the Sun alternately make Earth's climate warmer and colder at time scales ranging from 100,000 years to 11,000 years. These cycles, known as *Milankovitch cycles,* have been convincingly shown to correlate with advances and retreats of the glaciers in the past few million years and have operated throughout Earth history.

Changes in ocean circulation patterns caused by changes in seawater salinity and many other factors can dramatically change the pattern of heat distribution on the planet and global climate. Many ocean currents are driven by differences in temperature and salinity of ocean waters, and these currents form a pattern of global circulation known as *thermohaline circulation.* Changes in patterns of thermohaline circulation can occur quite rapidly, perhaps even over 5–10 years, suddenly plunging warm continents into long icy winters, or warming frozen ice-covered landscapes. Other changes in the ocean-atmosphere system cause the local climate to change on 5–10 year time scales, and the most dramatic of these is the *El Niño*–Southern Oscillation that strongly affects the Pacific and Americas but has influences worldwide.

Astronomical Forcing of the Climate

Medium-term climate changes include those that alternate between warm and cold on time scales of 100,000 years or less. These medium term climate changes include the semi-regular advance and retreat of the glaciers during the many individual ice ages in the past few million years. The last 2.8 Ma have been marked by large global climate oscillations that have been recurring at approximately a 100,000 year periodicity at least for the past 800,000 years. The warm periods, called interglacial periods, appear to last approximately 15,000 to 20,000 years before regressing back to a cold ice age climate. The last of these major glacial intervals began ending about 18,000 years ago, as the large continental ice sheets covering North America, Europe, and Asia began retreating. The main climate events related to the retreat of the glaciers, can be summarized as follows:

- 18,000 years ago: the climate begins to warm
- 15,000 years ago: advance of glaciers halts and sea levels begin to rise
- 10,000 years ago: Ice Age megafauna goes extinct
- 8,000 years ago: Bering Strait land bridge becomes drowned, cutting off migration of people and animals
- 6,000 years ago: The Holocene maximum warm period
- So far in the past 18,000 years, Earth's temperature has risen approximately 16°F (10°C) and the sea level has risen 300 feet (91 m).

This past glacial retreat is but one of many in the past several million years, with an alternation of warm and cold periods apparently related to a 100,000 year periodicity in the amount of incoming solar radiation, causing the alternating warm and cold intervals. Systematic changes in the amount of incoming solar radiation, caused by variations in Earth's orbital parameters around the Sun, are known as Milankovitch cycles, after Milutin Milankovitch (1879–1958), a Serbian scientist who first clearly elucidated the relationships between the astronomical variations of Earth orbiting the Sun and the climate cycles on Earth. These changes can affect many Earth systems, causing glaciations, global warming, and changes in the patterns of climate and sedimentation. Milankovitch's main scientific work was published by the Royal Academy of Serbia in 1941, during World War II in Europe. He was able to calculate that the effects of orbital *eccentricity, wobble,* and *tilt* combine every 40,000 years to change the amount of incoming solar radiation, lowering temperatures and causing increased snowfall at high latitudes. His results have been widely used to interpret climatic variations, especially in the Pleistocene record of ice ages, and also in the older rock record.

Astronomical effects influence the amount of incoming solar radiation; minor variations in the path of Earth in its orbit around the Sun and the inclination or tilt of its axis cause variations in the amount of

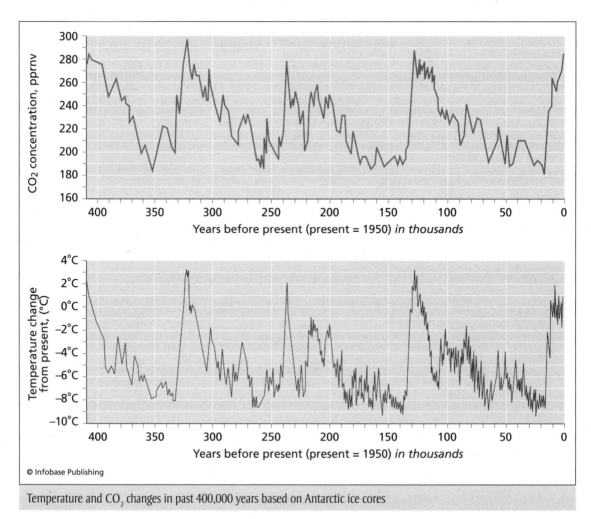

Temperature and CO_2 changes in past 400,000 years based on Antarctic ice cores

solar energy reaching the top of the atmosphere. These variations are thought to be responsible for the advance and retreat of the Northern and Southern Hemisphere ice sheets in the past few million years. In

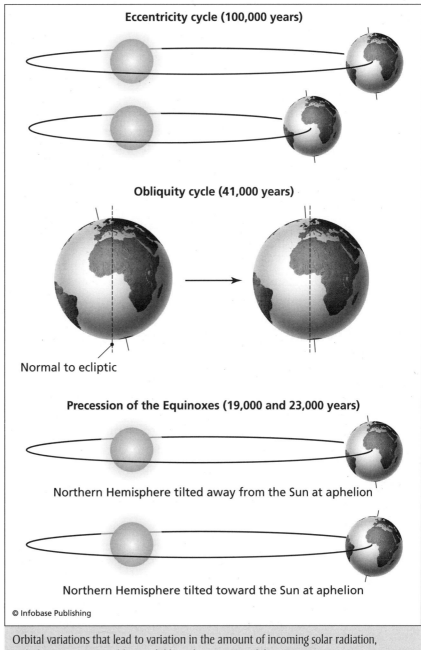

Eccentricity cycle (100,000 years)

Obliquity cycle (41,000 years)

Normal to ecliptic

Precession of the Equinoxes (19,000 and 23,000 years)

Northern Hemisphere tilted away from the Sun at aphelion

Northern Hemisphere tilted toward the Sun at aphelion

© Infobase Publishing

Orbital variations that lead to variation in the amount of incoming solar radiation, including eccentricity, obliquity (tilt), and precession of the equinoxes

the past two million years alone, Earth has seen the ice sheets advance and retreat approximately 20 times. The climate record as deduced from ice-core records from Greenland and isotopic tracer studies from deep ocean, lake, and cave sediments suggests that the ice builds up gradually over periods of about 100,000 years, then retreats rapidly over a period of decades to a few thousand years. These patterns result from the cumulative effects of different astronomical phenomena.

Several movements are involved in changing the amount of incoming solar radiation. Earth rotates around the Sun following an elliptical orbit, and the shape of this elliptical orbit is known as its eccentricity. The eccentricity changes cyclically with time with a period of 100,000 years, alternately bringing Earth closer to and farther from the Sun in summer and winter. This 100,000-year cycle is about the same as the general pattern of glaciers advancing and retreating every 100,000 years in the past two million years, suggesting that this is the main cause of variations within the present day ice age. Presently, we are in a period of low eccentricity (~3 percent) and this gives us a seasonal change in solar energy of ~7 percent. When the eccentricity is at its peak (~9 percent), "seasonality" reaches ~20 percent. In addition, a more eccentric orbit changes the length of seasons in each hemisphere by changing the length of time between the vernal and autumnal equinoxes.

Earth's axis is presently tilting by 23.5°N/S away from the orbital plane, and the tilt varies between 21.5°N/S and 24.5°N/S. The tilt, also known as obliquity, changes by plus or minus 1.5°N/S from a tilt of 23°N/S every 41,000 years. When the tilt is greater, there is greater seasonal variation in temperature. For small tilts, the winters would tend to be milder and the summers cooler. This would lead to more glaciation.

Wobble of the rotation axis describes a motion much like a top rapidly spinning and rotating with a wobbling motion, such that the direction of tilt toward or away from the Sun changes, even though the tilt amount stays the same. This wobbling phenomenon is known as precession of the equinoxes, and it has the effect of placing different hemispheres closest to the Sun in different seasons. This precession changes with a double cycle, with periodicities of 23,000 years and 19,000 years. Presently the precession of the equinoxes is such that Earth is closest

(Opposite) Milankovitch cycles related to changes in eccentricity, obliquity (tilt), and precession of the equinoxes. All of these effects act together, and the curves need to be added to each other to obtain a true accurate curve of the climate variations due to all of these effects acting at the same time.

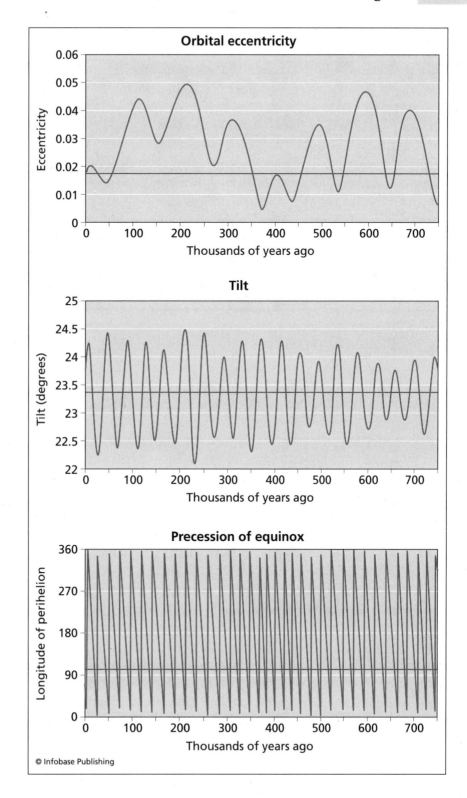

Butterloch Canyon, Dolomites, Italy, showing cyclic layering interpreted as reflecting different environmental conditions caused by Milankovitch cycles *(CORBIS)*

to the Sun during the Northern Hemisphere winter. Due to precession, the reverse will be true in ~11,000 years. This will give the Northern Hemisphere more severe winters.

Because these astronomical factors act on different time scales, they interact in a complicated way, known as Milankovitch cycles, after Milutin Milankovitch. Using the power of understanding these cycles, we can make predictions of where Earth's climate is heading, whether we are heading into a warming or cooling period, and whether we need to plan for sea level rise, desertification, glaciation, sea level drops, floods, or droughts. When all the Milankovitch cycles (alone) are taken into account, the present trend should be toward a cooler climate in the Northern Hemisphere, with extensive glaciation. The Milankovitch cycles may help explain the advance and retreat of ice over periods of 10,000 to 100,000 years. They do not explain what caused the Ice Age in the first place.

The pattern of climate cycles predicted by Milankovitch cycles is made more complex by other factors that change the climate of Earth. These include changes in thermohaline circulation, changes in the amount of dust in the atmosphere, changes caused by reflectivity of ice sheets, changes in concentration of greenhouse gases, changing characteristics of clouds, and even the *glacial rebound* of land that was depressed below sea level by the weight of glaciers.

Milankovitch cycles have been invoked to explain the rhythmic repetitions of layers in some sedimentary rock sequences. The cyclical orbital variations cause cyclical climate variations, which in turn are reflected in the cyclical deposition of specific types of sedimentary layers in sensitive environments. There are numerous examples of sedimentary sequences where stratigraphic and age control are sufficient to be able to detect cyclical variation on the time scales of Milankovitch cycles, and studies of these layers have proven consistent with a control of sedimentation by the planet's orbital variations. Some examples of Milankovitch-forced sedimentation have been documented from the Dolomite Mountains of Italy, the Proterozoic Rocknest Formation of northern Canada, and from numerous coral *reef* environments.

Predicting the future climate on Earth involves very complex calculations, including input from the long- and medium-term effects described in this chapter and some short-term effects, such as sudden changes caused by human input of greenhouse gases to the atmosphere and effects such as unpredicted volcanic eruptions. Nonetheless, most climate experts expect that the planet will continue to warm on the hundreds-of-years time scale. However, based on the recent geological past, it seems reasonable that the planet could be suddenly plunged into another ice age, perhaps initiated by sudden changes in ocean circulation, following a period of warming. Climate is one of the major drivers of *mass extinction,* so the question remains if the human race will be able to cope with rapidly fluctuating temperatures, dramatic changes in sea level, and enormous shifts in climate and agriculture belts.

Thermohaline Circulation and Climate

Variations in formation and circulation of ocean water may cause some of the thousands of years to decadal scale variations in climate. Cold water forms in the Arctic and Weddell Seas. This cold salty water is denser than other water in the ocean, so it sinks to the bottom and gets ponded behind seafloor topographic ridges, periodically spilling over into other parts of the oceans. The formation and redistribution of North Atlantic cold bottom water accounts for about 30 percent of the solar energy budget input to the Arctic Ocean every year. Eventually, this cold bottom water works its way to the Indian and Pacific Oceans where it upwells, gets heated, and returns to the North Atlantic. Thermohaline circulation is the vertical mixing of seawater driven by density differences caused by variations in temperature and salinity. Variations

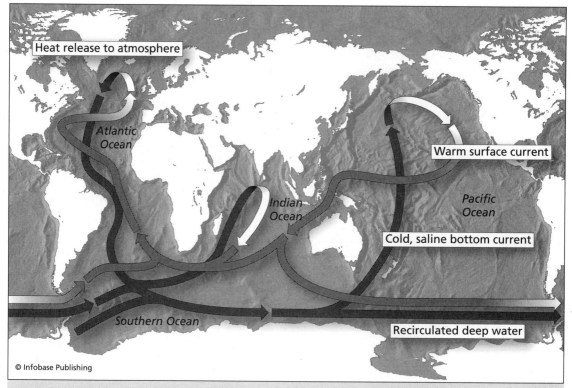

Map of the world's oceans showing main warm and cold currents driven by thermohaline circulation

in temperature and salinity are found in waters that occupy different ocean basins and those found at different levels in the water column. When the density of water at one level is greater than or equal to that below that level, the water column becomes unstable and the denser water sinks, displacing the deeper, less-dense waters below. When the dense water reaches the level at which it is stable it tends to spread out laterally and form a thin sheet, forming intricately stratified ocean waters. Thermohaline circulation is the main mechanism responsible for the movement of water out of cold polar regions and exerts a strong influence on global climate. The upward movement of water in other regions balances the sinking of dense cold water, and these upwelling regions typically bring deep water, rich in nutrients, to the surface. Thus, regions of intense biological activity are often associated with upwelling regions.

The coldest water on the planet is formed in the polar regions, with large quantities of cold water originating off the coast of Greenland and in the Weddell Sea of Antarctica. The planet's saltiest ocean water is found in the Atlantic Ocean, and this is moved northward by the Gulf Stream. As this water moves near Greenland it is cooled and then sinks to flow as a deep cold current along the bottom of the western North Atlantic. The cold water of the Weddell Sea is the densest on the planet, where surface waters are cooled to $-35.4°F$ ($-1.9°C$), then sink to form a cold current that moves around Antarctica. Some of this deep cold water moves northward into all three major ocean basins, mixing with other waters and warming slightly. Most of these deep ocean currents move at one to four inches (a few to 10 cm) per second.

Presently, the age of bottom water in the equatorial Pacific is 1,600 years, and in the Atlantic it is 350 years. Glacial stages in the North Atlantic have been correlated with the presence of older cold bottom waters, approximately twice the age of the water today. This suggests that the thermohaline circulation system was only half as effective at recycling water during recent glacial stages, with less cold bottom water being produced during the glacial periods. These changes in production of cold bottom water may in turn be driven by changes in the North American ice sheet, perhaps itself driven by 23,000 year orbital (Milankovitch) cycles. It is thought that a growth in the ice sheet would cause the polar front to shift southward, decreasing the inflow of cold saline surface water into the system required for efficient thermohaline circulation. Several periods of glaciation in the past 14,500 years (known as the Dryas) are thought to have been caused by sudden, even catastrophic, injections into the North Atlantic of glacial meltwater that would decrease the salinity and hence density of the surface water. This in turn would prohibit the surface water from sinking to the deep ocean, inducing another glacial interval.

Shorter-term decadal variations in climate in the past million years are indicated by so-called *Heinrich Events*, defined as specific intervals in the sedimentary record showing ice-rafted debris in the North Atlantic. These periods of exceptionally large iceberg discharges reflect decadal scale sea surface and atmospheric cooling related to thickening of the North American ice sheet followed by ice stream surges. These events flood the surface waters with low-salinity fresh water, leading to a decrease in flux to the cold bottom waters, and hence a short period global cooling.

Changes in the thermohaline circulation rigor have also been related to other global climate changes. Droughts in the Sahel and elsewhere are correlated with periods of ineffective or reduced thermohaline circulation, because this reduces the amount of water drawn into the

North Atlantic, in turn cooling surface waters and reducing the amount of evaporation. Reduced thermohaline circulation also reduces the amount of water that upwells in the equatorial regions, in turn decreasing the amount of moisture transferred to the atmosphere, reducing precipitation at high latitudes.

Atmospheric levels of greenhouse gases such as CO_2 and atmospheric temperatures show a correlation to variations in the thermohaline circulation patterns and production of cold bottom waters. CO_2 is dissolved in warm surface water and transported to cold surface water, which acts as a sink for the CO_2. During times of decreased flow from cold, high-latitude surface water to the deep ocean reservoir, CO_2 can build up in the cold polar waters, removing it from the atmosphere and decreasing global temperatures. In contrast, when the thermohaline circulation is vigorous, cold oxygen-rich surface waters downwell, and dissolve buried CO_2 and even carbonates, releasing this CO_2 to the atmosphere and increasing global temperatures.

The present day ice sheet in Antarctica grew in the middle Miocene, related to active thermohaline circulation that caused prolific upwelling of warm water that put more moisture in the atmosphere, falling as snow on the cold southern continent. The growth of the southern ice sheet increased the global atmospheric temperature gradients, which in turn increased the desertification of mid-latitude continental regions. The increased temperature gradient also induced stronger oceanic circulation, including upwelling and removal of CO_2 from the atmosphere, lowering global temperatures and bringing on late Neogene glaciations.

Ocean bottom topography exerts a strong influence on dense bottom currents. Ridges deflect currents from one part of a basin to another and may restrict access to other regions, whereas trenches and deeps may focus flow from one region to another.

El Niño and the Southern Oscillation (ENSO)

El Niño–Southern Oscillation is the name given to one of the better-known variations in global atmospheric circulation patterns. Global oceanic and atmospheric circulation patterns undergo frequent shifts that affect large parts of the globe, particularly those arid and semi-arid parts affected by Hadley Cell circulation. It is now understood that fluctuations in global circulation can account for natural disasters, including the dust bowl days of the 1930s in the midwestern United States. Similar global climate fluctuations may explain the drought, famine, and desertification of parts of the Sahel and the great famines of Ethiopia and Sudan in the 1970s and 1980s.

The secondary air circulation phenomenon known as the El Niño–Southern Oscillation can also have profound influences on the development of drought conditions and desertification of stressed lands. Hadley Cells migrate north and south with summer and winter, shifting the locations of the most intense heating. There are several zonal oceanic-

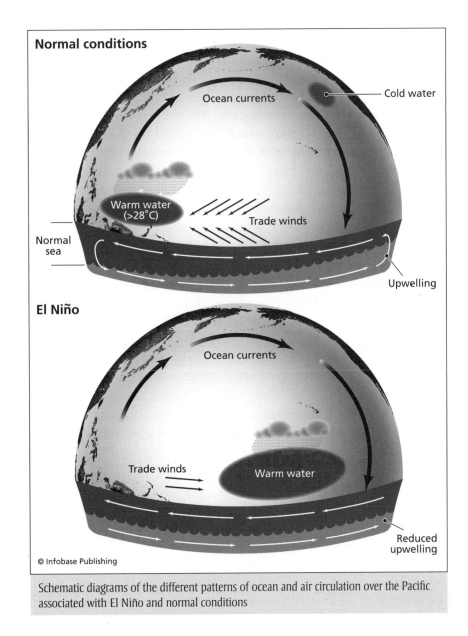

Schematic diagrams of the different patterns of ocean and air circulation over the Pacific associated with El Niño and normal conditions

atmospheric feedback systems that influence global climate, but the most influential is that of the Australasian system. In normal Northern Hemisphere summers, the location of the most intense heating in Australasia shifts from equatorial regions to the Indian subcontinent along with the start of the Indian *monsoon*. Air is drawn onto the subcontinent, where it rises and moves outward to Africa and the central Pacific. In Northern Hemisphere winters, the location of this intense heating shifts to Indonesia and Australia, where an intense low-pressure system develops over this mainly maritime region. Air is sucked in and moves upward and flows back out at tropospheric levels to the east Pacific. High pressure develops off the coast of Peru in both situations, because cold upwelling water off the coast here causes the air to cool, inducing atmospheric downwelling. The pressure gradient set up causes easterly trade winds to blow from the coast of Peru across the Pacific to the region of heating, causing warm water to pile up in the Coral Sea off the northeast coast of Australia. This also causes sea level to be slightly depressed off the coast of Peru, and more cold water upwells from below to replace the lost water. This positive feedback mechanism is rather stable—it enhances the global circulation, as more cold water upwelling off Peru induces more atmospheric downwelling, and more warm water piling up in Indonesia and off the coast of Australia causes atmospheric upwelling in this region.

This stable linked atmospheric and oceanic circulation breaks down and becomes unstable every two to seven years, probably from some inherent chaotic behavior in the system. At these times, the Indonesian-Australian heating center migrates eastward, and the build-up of warm water in the western Pacific is no longer held back by winds blowing westward across the Pacific. This causes the elevated warm water mass to collapse and move eastward across the Pacific, where it typically appears off the coast of Peru by the end of December. The El Niño–Southern Oscillation (ENSO) events occur when this warming is particularly strong, with temperatures increasing by 40–43°F (22–24°C) and remaining high for several months. This phenomenon is also associated with a reversal of the atmospheric circulation around the Pacific such that the dry downwelling air is located over Australia and Indonesia, and the warm upwelling air is located over the eastern Pacific and western South America.

The arrival of El Niño is not good news in Peru, since it causes the normally cold upwelling and nutrient rich water to sink to great depths, and the fish either must migrate to better feeding locations or die. The

View of the remains of the town of Santa Teresa, Peru, 310 miles (500 km) southeast of Lima in the Andes. The town was devastated by mud and rock flows from the Sacsara River, which overflowed from heavy rains associated with El Niño, killing 17 people and leaving 1,000 homeless. *(AP)*

fishing industry collapses at these times, as does the fertilizer industry that relies on the bird guano normally produced by birds (that eat fish and anchovies) that also die during El Niño events. The normally cold dry air is replaced with warm moist air and the normally dry or desert regions of coastal Peru receive torrential rains with associated floods, *landslides,* death, and destruction. Shoreline erosion is accelerated in El Niño events, because the warm water mass that moved in from across the Pacific raises sea levels by 4–25 inches (10–60 cm), enough to cause significant damage.

The end of ENSO events also leads to abnormal conditions, in that they seem to turn on the "normal" type of circulation in a much stronger way than is normal. The cold upwelling water returns off Peru with such a ferocity that it may move northward, flooding a 1–2° band around the equator in the central Pacific ocean with water that is as cold as 68°F (20° C). This phenomenon is known as La Niña ("the girl" in Spanish).

The alternation between ENSO, La Niña, and normal ocean-atmospheric circulation has profound effects on global climate and the migration of different climate belts on yearly to decadal time scales, and is thought to account for about a third of all the variability in global rainfall. ENSO events may cause flooding in the western Andes and southern

California and a lack of rainfall in other parts of South America including Venezuela, northeastern Brazil, and southern Peru. It may change the climate, causing droughts in Africa, Indonesia, India, and Australia and is thought to have caused the failure of the Indian monsoon in 1899 that resulted in regional famine with the deaths of millions of people. Recently, the seven-year cycle of floods on the Nile has been linked to ENSO events, and famine and desertification in the Sahel, Ethiopia, and Sudan can be attributed to these changes in global circulation as well.

Major Volcanic Eruptions and Climate Change

Some of the larger, more explosive volcanic eruptions that the planet has witnessed in the past few hundred years have ejected large amounts of ash and finer particles called aerosols into the atmosphere and stratosphere, and it may take years for these particles to settle back down to Earth. They get distributed about the planet by high-level winds, and they have the effect of blocking out some of the Sun's rays, which lowers global temperatures. This happens because particles and *aerosol* gases in the upper atmosphere tend to scatter sunlight back to space, lowering the amount of incoming solar energy. In contrast, particles that get injected into only the lower atmosphere absorb sunlight and contribute to greenhouse warming. A side effect is that the extra particles in the atmosphere also produce more spectacular sunsets and sunrises, as does extra pollution in the atmosphere. These effects were readily observed after the 1991 eruption of Mount Pinatubo, which spewed more than 172 billion cubic feet (5 billion m³) of ash and aerosols into the atmosphere, causing global cooling for two years after the eruption. Even more spectacularly, the 1815 eruption of Tambora in Indonesia caused three days of total darkness for approximately 300 miles (500 km) from the volcano, and it initiated the famous "year without a summer" in Europe, because the ash from this eruption lowered global temperatures by more than a degree.

The amounts of gases and small airborne particles released by large volcanic eruptions such as Pinatubo and Tambora are dwarfed by the amount of material placed into the atmosphere during some of Earth's most massive eruptions, known as *flood basalt* events. No flood basalts have been formed on Earth for several tens of millions of years, which is a good thing, since their eruption may be associated with severe changes in climate.

Scattered around the globe are numerous anomalously thick accumulations of dark *lava*, variously known as flood basalts, traps, or large igneous provinces. These vast outpourings of lava have different ages and represent the largest known volcanic episodes on the planet in the past several hundred million years. These deposits include continental flood basalt provinces, anomalously thick and topographically high seafloor known as oceanic plateaus, and some volcanic rifted passive margins.

UNDERSTANDING THE GREENHOUSE EFFECT

The term *greenhouse effect* refers to a phenomenon where Earth's climate is sensitive to the concentrations of certain gases in the atmosphere. The concept was first coined in 1681 by Edme Mariotte, who noted that light and heat from the Sun easily passes through a sheet of glass but that heat from candles and other sources does not. This concept was then extended by Joseph Fourier in 1824 to the atmosphere by noting that heat and light from the Sun can pass from space through the atmosphere, but heat radiated back to the atmosphere from Earth may get trapped by some of the atmospheric gases, just like the heat from a candle is partly blocked by the glass pane. Then in 1861 John Tyndall identified that the complex molecules of water (H_2O) and carbon dioxide (CO_2) were mainly responsible for the absorption of heat radiated back from Earth and that other atmospheric gases such as nitrogen and oxygen did not play a role in this effect. Tyndall noted that simple changes in the concentrations of CO_2 and H_2O could alternately cool and heat the atmosphere, producing "all the mutations of climate which the researches of geologists reveal." The next step in understanding the greenhouse effect came in 1896 from the work of Svante Arrhenius, who calculated that a 40 percent increase or decrease in the atmospheric concentration of CO_2 could trigger the advance and or retreat of continental glaciers, triggering the glacial and interglacial ages. Much later, a change in the atmospheric CO_2 of this magnitude was documented in cores of the Greenland ice sheet, as predicted by Arrhenius. Carbon dioxide can vary naturally in the atmosphere through a variety of driving mechanisms, including changes in volcanism, erosion, plate tectonics, and ocean-atmosphere interactions. The modern concept of linking greenhouse gases with the burning of fossil fuels by humans was formulated by Guy Stewart Callendar, who in 1938 calculated that a doubling of atmospheric CO_2 by burning fossil fuels would result in an average global temperature increase of about 3°F (2°C), with more heating at the poles. Callendar made some prescient predictions that humans are changing the composition of the atmosphere at a rate that is "exceptional" on geological time scales and sought to understand what effects these changes might have on climate. His prediction was that the "principal result of increasing carbon dioxide will be a gradual increase in the mean temperature of the colder regions of Earth." These predictions were first confirmed in 1947 when Ahlmann reported a 1–2°F (1.3°C) increase in the average temperature of the North Atlantic sector of the Arctic. However, at this time the nature of the complex interactions of the carbon cycle and exchange of CO_2 in the atmosphere-ocean system was not well understood, and many scientists attributed the entire temperature rise to human production of greenhouse gases. Later studies of ocean-atmosphere relationships and biogeochemistry showed more complex relationships. Later, in the 1970s, effects of aerosols in the atmosphere, principally to reflect solar radiation to space and cooling Earth, began to be appreciated as another component of the greenhouse effect. The current state of knowledge of the complex physical, chemical, biological and other processes associated with the greenhouse effect are described in the "Climate Change 2007" report issued by the Intergovernmental Panel on Climate Change.

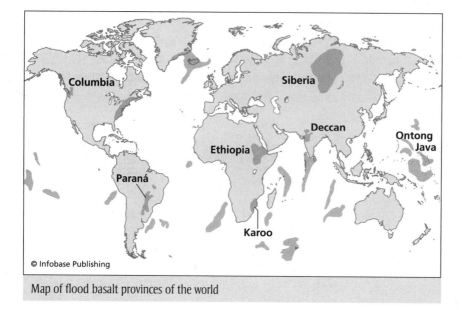

Map of flood basalt provinces of the world

During eruption of these vast piles of volcanic rock Earth moved more material and energy from its interior in extremely short time periods than during the entire intervals between the massive volcanic events. Such large amounts of volcanism also released large amounts of volcanic gases into the atmosphere, with serious implications for global temperatures and climate, and may have contributed to some global mass extinctions. Many are associated with periods of global cooling where volcanic gases reduce the amount of incoming solar radiation, resulting in volcanic winters.

The largest continental flood basalt province in the United States is the Columbia River flood basalt in Washington, Oregon, and Idaho. The Columbia River flood basalt province is 6–17 million years old, and contains an estimated 1,250 cubic miles (5,210 km³) of basalt. Individual lava flows erupted through fissures or cracks in the crust; it then flowed laterally across the plain for up to 400 miles.

The 66-million-year-old Deccan flood basalts, also known as traps, cover a large part of western India and the Seychelles. They are associated with the breakup of India from the Seychelles during the opening of the Indian Ocean. Slightly older flood basalts (90–83 million years old) are associated with the breakaway of Madagascar from India. The volume of the Deccan traps is estimated at 5,000,000 cubic miles (20,840,000 km³), and the volcanics are thought to have been erupted in about 1 million years, starting slightly before the great Cretaceous-Tertiary extinction. Most workers now agree that the gases released during this period of flood basalt volcanism stressed the global biosphere to such an extent that many marine organisms were forced into extinction, and many others were stressed. Then the planet was hit by the meteorite that formed the massive Chicxulub impact crater on the Yucatán Peninsula (Mexico), causing the massive extinction including the end of the dinosaurs.

The breakup of east Africa along the East African rift system and the Red Sea is associated with large amounts of Cenozoic (less than 30 million years old) continental flood basalts. Some of the older volcanic fields are located in east Africa in the Afar region of Ethiopia, south into Kenya and Uganda, and north across the Red Sea and Gulf of Aden into Yemen and Saudi Arabia. These volcanic piles are overlain by younger (less than 15 million-year-old) flood basalts that extend both farther south into Tanzania and farther north through central Arabia, where they are known as Harrats, and into Syria, Israel, Lebanon, and Jordan.

An older volcanic province also associated with the breakup of a continent is known as the North Atlantic Igneous Province. It formed along with the breakup of the North Atlantic Ocean at 62–55 million years ago and includes both onshore and offshore volcanic flows and intrusions in Greenland, Iceland, and the northern British Isles, including most of the Rockall Plateau and Faeroe Islands. In the South Atlantic, a similar 129–134 million-year-old flood basalt was split by the opening of the ocean and now has two parts. In Brazil, the flood lavas are known as the Paraná basalts, and in Namibia and Angola of West Africa as the Etendeka basalts.

The Caribbean Sea floor represents one of the best examples of an oceanic plateau, with other major examples including the Ontong-Java Plateau, Manihiki Plateau, Hess Rise, Shatsky Rise, and Mid-Pacific Mountains. All of these oceanic plateaus contain between six- and 25-mile- (9- and 40 km-) thick piles of volcanic and subvolcanic rocks representing huge outpourings of lava. The Caribbean Sea floor preserves 5–13 mile (8–21 km) thick oceanic crust formed before about 85 million years ago in the eastern Pacific Ocean. This unusually thick ocean floor was transported eastward by plate tectonics, where pieces of the seafloor collided with South America as it passed into the Atlantic Ocean. Pieces of the Caribbean oceanic crust are now preserved in Colombia, Ecuador, Panama, Hispanolia, and Cuba, and some scientists estimate that the Caribbean oceanic plateau may have once been twice its present size. In either case, it represents a vast outpouring of lava

Photo of limestone rocks, deposited in a shallow sea in the Carboniferous (300 million years ago) on shoreline of Fayette Village State Park, Michigan, showing how climate and sea level rise have at times in Earth history raised sea levels so that much of the continental interior is covered by shallow seas. *(CORBIS)*

that would have been associated with significant outgassing with possible consequences for global climate and evolution.

The western Pacific Ocean basin contains several large oceanic plateaus, including the 20 mile (32 km) thick crust of the Alaskan-sized Ontong-Java Plateau, which is the largest outpouring of volcanic rocks on the planet. It apparently formed in two intervals, at 122 and 90 million years ago, entirely within the ocean, and represents magma that rose in a plume from deep in the mantle and erupted on the seafloor. It is estimated that the volume of magma erupted in the first event was equivalent to that of all the magma being erupted at mid-ocean ridges at the present time. Sea levels rose by more than 30 feet (9 m) in response to this volcanic outpouring. The gases released during these eruptions are estimated to have raised average global temperatures by 23°F (13°C).

Examples of Climate Changes Caused by Flood Basalt Volcanism

The environmental impact of the eruption of large volumes of basalt can be severe. Huge volumes of sulfur dioxide, carbon dioxide, chlorine, and fluorine are released during large basaltic eruptions. Much of this gas may get injected into the upper troposphere and lower stratosphere during the eruption process, being released from eruption columns that reach two to eight miles (3–13 km) in height. Carbon dioxide is a greenhouse gas, and can cause global warming, whereas sulfur dioxide and hydrogen sulfate have the opposite effect and can cause short-term cooling. Many of the episodes of volcanism preserved in these large igneous provinces were rapid, repeatedly releasing enormous quantities of gases over periods of less than one million years, and released enough gas to significantly change the climate more rapidly than organisms could adapt to these changes. For instance, one eruption of the Colombia River basalts is estimated to have released 9 billion tons of sulfur dioxide, and thousands of millions of tons of other gases, compared to the eruption of Mount Pinatubo in 1991, which released about 20 million tons of sulfur dioxide.

The Colombia River basalts of the Pacific Northwest are instructive about how flood basalts can influence climate. These lavas continued erupting for years at a time, for approximately a million years. During this time the gases released would be equivalent to that of Mount Pinatubo every week over periods maintained for decades to thousands of years at a time. The atmospheric consequences are sobering. Sulfuric acid aerosols and acid from the fluorine and chlorine would form extensive poisonous acid rain, destroying habitats and making waters uninhabitable for some organisms. At the very least, the environmental consequences would be such that organisms were stressed to the point that they would not be able to handle an additional environmental stress, such as a global volcanic winter and subsequent warming caused by a giant impact.

Mass extinctions have been correlated with the eruption of the Deccan flood basalts at the Cretaceous-Tertiary (K/T) boundary and with the Siberian flood basalts at the Permian-Triassic boundary. There is still considerable debate about the relative significance of flood basalt volcanism and impacts of meteorites for extinction events, particularly at the Cretaceous-Tertiary boundary. However, most scientists would now agree that global environment was stressed shortly before the K/T boundary by volcanic-induced climate change, and then a huge meteorite hit the Yucatan Peninsula, forming the Chicxulub impact crater, causing the massive K/T boundary extinction and the death of the dinosaurs.

The Siberian flood basalts cover a large area of the Central Siberian Plateau northwest of Lake Baikal. They are more than half a mile thick over an area of 210,000 square miles (543,900 km^2) but have been significantly eroded from an estimated volume of 1,240,000 cubic miles (3,211,600 km^3). They were erupted over an extraordinarily short period of less than 1 million years 250 million years ago, at the Permian-Triassic boundary. They are remarkably coincident in time with the major Permian-Triassic extinction, implying a causal link. The Permian-Triassic boundary at 250 million years ago marks the greatest extinction in Earth history, where 90 percent of marine species and 70 percent of terrestrial vertebrates became extinct. It has been postulated that the rapid volcanism and degassing released enough sulfur dioxide to cause a rapid global cooling, inducing a short ice age with associated rapid fall of sea level. Soon after the ice age took hold the effects of the carbon dioxide took over and the atmosphere heated, resulting in a global warming. The rapidly fluctuating climate postulated to have been caused by the volcanic gases is thought to have killed off many organisms, which were simply unable to cope with the wildly fluctuating climate extremes.

The close relationship between massive volcanism and changes in climate that have led to mass extinctions shows how quickly life on Earth can change. The effects of massive global volcanism are much larger than any changes so far caused by humans and operate faster than other plate tectonic and supercontinent related changes.

How Fast Can Climate Change?

Understanding how fast climate can shift from a warm period to a cold, or cold to a warm, is difficult. The record of climate indicators is incomplete and difficult to interpret. Only 18,000 years ago the planet was in the midst of a major glacial interval, and since then global average temperatures have risen 16°F (10°C) and are still rising, perhaps at a recently accelerated rate from human contributions to the atmosphere. Still, recent climate work is revealing that there are some abrupt transitions in the slow warming in which there are major shifts in some component of the climate, where the shift may happen on scales of ten years or less.

One of these abrupt transitions seems to affect the ocean circulation pattern in the North Atlantic Ocean, where the ocean currents formed one of two different stable patterns or modes, with abrupt transitions occurring when one mode switches to the other. In the present pattern the warm waters of the Gulf Stream come out of the Gulf of Mexico and flow along the eastern seaboard of the United States, past the British

Isles, to the Norwegian Sea. This warm current is largely responsible for the mild climate of the British Isles and northern Europe. In the second mode, the northern extension of the Gulf Stream is weakened by a reduction in salinity of surface waters from sources at high latitudes in the North Atlantic. The fresher water has a source in increased melting from the polar ice shelf, Greenland, and northern glaciers. With less salt, seawater is less dense, and is less able to sink during normal wintertime cooling.

Studies of past switches in the circulation modes of the North Atlantic reveal that the transition from mode 1 to mode 2 can occur over a period of only five to ten years. These abrupt transitions are apparently linked to increases in the release of icebergs and freshwater from continental glaciers, which upon melting contribute large volumes of freshwater into the North Atlantic, systematically reducing the salinity. The Gulf Stream presently seems on the verge of failure, or of switching modes from mode 1 to 2, and historical records show that this switch can be very rapid. If this predicted switch occurs, northern Europe and the United Kingdom may experience a significant and dramatic cooling of their climate, instead of the warming many fear.

Conclusion

Earth's climate exhibits natural variations on time scales of years to hundreds of thousands of years because of variations in a number of climate-forcing factors. Variations in Earth's orbit around the Sun can change the amount of incoming solar radiation. The shape or eccentricity of Earth's orbit around the Sun changes with a cycle of 100,000 years, leading to alternating warmer and colder periods on Earth. The obliquity of the tilt of the rotational axis alternates with a frequency of 41,000 years, also leading to variations in the amount of incoming solar radiation in different hemispheres in different seasons. The precession, or direction that the tilt axis is inclined relative to the Sun in different seasons, changes with two frequencies of 19,000 and 23,000 years. Together, these astronomical climate-forcing mechanisms are responsible for many of the variations in Earth's climate in geological time. These cycles interact in a complex way, producing a sequence of warm and cold climate phases known as Milankovitch Cycles.

Thermohaline, or temperature and salinity driven, circulation of the world's oceans also exhibits a strong control on climate. When the patterns of thermohaline circulation change, from changes in the distribution of continents, in salinity, or in climate caused by other factors, then the pattern of ocean circulation can suddenly change, plunging regions into dramatically different climate patterns in very short times.

The El Niño–Southern Oscillation refers to a variation in a global variation in atmospheric circulation in the Austro-Pacific realm that affects the entire globe. This circulation pattern is caused by alternate heating in the Indonesian-Australian region and drives warm and cold water back and forth across the Pacific in an narrow equatorial belt, strongly affecting the climate of western South and North America and changing global climate patterns on yearly to decadal time scales.

Major volcanic eruptions can suddenly change global climate, with effects that typically last for several years. The volcanic effect can cause heating by injection of CO_2 and other greenhouse gases to the atmosphere, or cooling by injection of ash and aerosols into the atmosphere. The most severe volcanic effects are those from the eruptions of giant igneous provinces called flood basalts, which can produce more volcanic material than is cumulatively being erupted along all of the planet's mid-ocean ridges. Massive volcanism can put so much carbon dioxide into the atmosphere that the temperature can warm by several degrees or more, placing the planet's ecosystems under a stressed condition, and lasting millions of years. Other flood basalt eruptions have placed so much dust and aerosols into the atmosphere they have cooled global climate by several degrees. Climate change induced by massive volcanism has played a major role in several of the mass extinction events in Earth history, including the major extinction that culminated in the death of the dinosaurs.

3

Human-Induced Climate Changes

Few scientists would disagree that the planet has been warming dramatically over the past century and that human contributions to climate change have been accelerating to critical levels as the world becomes increasingly industrialized. Much of what is known about these short-term climate changes has been described in a report issued in late 2007 by the Intergovernmental Panel on Climate Change, an international group of hundreds of scientists who have analyzed all available data, assessed the causes of these recent, short-term changes to the global climate, and made predictions of what the climate of Earth may look like at various times in the future. Much of the information in this chapter is based on the findings of the Intergovernmental Panel on Climate Change.

Eleven of the 12 years between 1996 and 2006 were the warmest on record since weather recording instruments were widely used starting in 1850. The rate of temperature increase seems to be increasing, with polar areas affected more than equatorial regions. Sea levels are also rising at an increasing rate. Between 1961 and 1993 global sea level was rising at a rate of .05–.09 inches per year (.13–.23 cm/yr.), and since 1993 they have been rising at .09–.11 inches per year (.24–.28 cm/yr.). Some of the sea level rise is due to melting glaciers, ice caps, and snow, and some is from thermal expansion of ocean water as the water warms. Glaciers are shrinking in both the Northern and Southern Hemispheres, and the ice caps on the Arctic Ocean and over parts of Antarctica are shrinking rapidly.

Global precipitation patterns are observably changing on the century scale, with much of eastern North and South America, northern Europe, and north and central Asia seeing increased rainfall but other areas such as the Sahel, Mediterranean, southern Africa, and southern Asia seeing decreased precipitation. On a global scale, areas that are experiencing drought or less precipitation are greater than areas receiving greater precipitation.

This chapter examines these and other trends in the short-term climate, focusing on changes since 1850, when the world was going through the later industrial revolution and people began increasing the amount of carbon dioxide and other greenhouse gases released into the atmosphere. Changes to different Earth systems are assessed, then possible causes of these changes are examined. Possible relative contributions of natural and man-made or anthropogenic changes are discussed, and different time-scales of climate forcing are presented.

Temperature Variations during the Past 1,000 Years

Understanding changes to Earth's climate in the past 100–200 years, or the slightly longer interval extending back through the last glacial interval, rely on several types of data. Instrumental records of Earth's climate extend back in time to about the year 1850, when recording devices were put into widespread use. Long cores of ice obtained from Greenland and other locations are also widely used to measure past climate conditions, with this record extending back for about 650,000 years.

The Intergovernmental Panel on Climate Change issued a statement in November 2007 that "warming of the climate system is unequivocal, as is now evident from observations of increases in global average air and ocean temperatures, widespread melting of snow and ice, and rising global average sea level." This bold statement was based on rigorous analysis of data from the past 1,000 years, showing that temperatures remained fairly steady at about 0–0.5 degrees below the 1990 average value from the year 1000 to about 1910, then began a sharp upward turn that flattened off for a short time in the 1950s and has turned sharply up again since about 1976. Temperatures are now about 0.5–1.0 degrees above the 1990 value and expected to rise 2–5 degrees above this value by 2100.

To measure global average temperatures, groups of meteorologists, such as the World Meteorological Organization (WMO) and the Global Climate Observing System (GCOS), have a large number

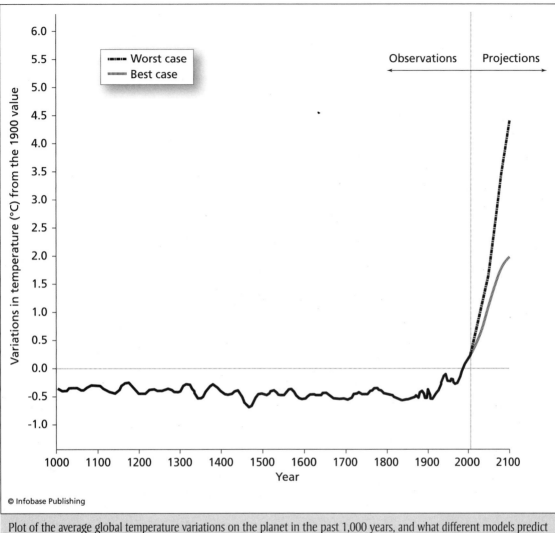

Plot of the average global temperature variations on the planet in the past 1,000 years, and what different models predict the temperature will be by the year 2100. All models show a predicted temperature rise, ranging between 1.5 and 5.5 degrees. *(IPCC 2007)*

of observation points on the continents, which are then gridded into equal areas to assign a temperature for each box in the grid. Where local observations are not available, and for calibrating the model, observations from satellites are widely used. Local effects, such as any *urban heat island* effect from cities, are accounted for in these types of models. With rapid improvements in computer modeling, it has been possible to make more and more detailed and accurate models for the globe.

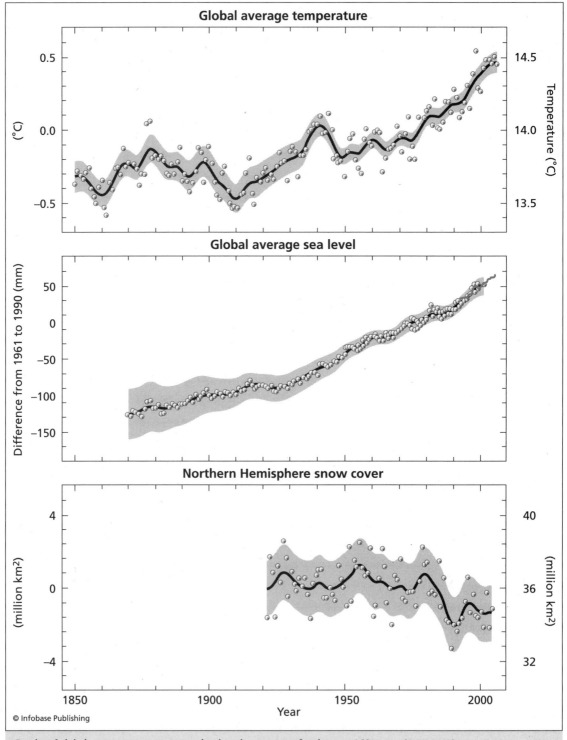

Graphs of global average temperature, sea level, and snow cover for the past 160 years *(IPCC 2007)*

© Infobase Publishing

Observed Short-term Climate Changes and Their Effects

Instrumental and ice core records show that several components of the atmosphere and surface have significant changes in recorded climate history. First, the concentration of greenhouse gases such as carbon dioxide has increased dramatically since 1850, causing an increase in the atmospheric absorption of outgoing radiation, warming the atmosphere. Aerosols, which are microscopic droplets or airborne particles, have also increased, and these have the effect of reflecting and absorbing incoming solar radiation.

The most obvious change to the short-term climate is the increase in temperature of the atmosphere and sea surface. Eleven of the 12 years between 1995 and 2006 rank among the hottest on record since instrumental records were in widespread use since 1850, with the rate of temperature rise increasing each interval since 1850. The total temperature increase since 1850 is estimated by the Intergovernmental Panel on Climate Change to be 1.4°F (0.76°C). Atmospheric water vapor has been measured to be increasing with increasing temperature of the atmosphere, although measurements of water vapor only extend back to about the middle 1980s.

Sea level has been rising at about .07 inches per year (.18 cm/yr.) since 1961, and at .12 inches per year (.31 cm/yr.) since 1993. The temperature of the oceans to a depth of 1.9 miles (3 km) has been increasing

Cornfield blighted by El Niño drought in Denton, Texas, July 22, 1998 *(CORBIS)*

since at least 1961, and most (~80 percent) of the heat energy associated with global warming is being absorbed by seawater. This increase in temperature of the seawater is causing the water to expand, contributing to sea level rise. Also contributing to sea level rise is a dramatic melting of mountain glaciers in both the Northern and Southern Hemispheres. Changes in the ice caps on Greenland and Antarctica show an increase in outflow of glacial ice and meltwater, so melting of the polar ice caps is very likely contributing to the measured sea level rise. Both of these ice caps show significant thinning, much due to increased melting, but some (especially on Greenland) due also to decreased snowfall.

Many specific regions of the planet are showing dramatic changes in response to the globally warming surface conditions. For instance, the surface temperatures measured in the Arctic have been increasing at about twice the global rate for the past 100 years, although some fluctuations on a decadal scale have been observed as well. The sea ice that covers the Arctic Ocean may be on the verge of collapse, as the sea ice thins and covers a smaller area each year. Since 1978 the Arctic sea ice has diminished in aerial extent by 2.7 percent each decade. On land in Arctic regions, the thick permafrost layer is also warming, by 4–5°F (~3°C), and a total decrease in the area covered by permafrost since 1900 estimated to be about 7 percent. Permafrost locks a huge amount of peat and carbon into a closed system, so there are fears that melting of the permafrost layer may release large amounts of carbon into the atmospheric system. The sea ice around Antarctica shows greater variations on interannual scales and no longer term trends are yet discernable. Much of the Antarctica region is isolated from other parts of the global climate belt, so overall, shows less change than northern polar regions.

Precipitation patterns across much of the planet are changing as a result of global warming. Observations from 1900 to 2005 show long-term drying and potential desertification over parts of the sub-Saharan Sahel, the Mediterranean region, parts of southern Asia, and southern Africa. Deeper and longer droughts have been occurring over larger areas since the 1970s, and some of these conditions can be related to changes in ocean temperature, wind patterns, and loss of snow cover. Westerly winds in the mid-latitudes have become stronger in both the Northern and Southern Hemispheres since the 1960s.

Weather extremes show an increase in frequency, including heavy precipitation events over land, as well as heat waves and extreme temperatures over land. Many studies suggest that oceanic *cyclones,* or hurricanes, may also be becoming stronger and more frequent, but some decadal variations in oceanic cyclones may also complicate determination of these trends. Most studies support an increase in tropical cyclone activity since the 1970s over the North Atlantic, and relate this to the increase in sea surface temperatures.

Causes of Short-term Climate Change

The Intergovernmental Panel on Climate Change issued new reports in 2007 which revealed that concentrations of some greenhouse gases have increased dramatically as a result of human activities, mostly starting with the early industrial revolution around 1750 and accelerating in the late industrial revolution around 1850. The greenhouse gases that show the most significant increases are carbon dioxide, methane, and nitrous oxide. Carbon dioxide (CO_2) is the most significant anthropogenic greenhouse gas and is produced mainly by burning of fossil fuels such as coal, oil, and gasoline. The atmospheric concentrations of CO_2 have increased from a pre-industrial revolution level of 280 parts per million (ppm) in the atmosphere to a 2005 level of 379 ppm, far exceeding the natural range (180–300 ppm) measured over the past 650,000 years, but CO_2 levels have been higher in the geological past for reasons related to global volcanism, supercontinent cycles, etc., that operate on longer time scales than the changes measured since the industrial revolution. Despite significant variations on a year-to-year basis, the rate of CO_2 increase in concentration in the atmosphere has been in acceleration over the past 10 years.

Methane in the atmosphere has increased in concentration from a pre-industrial revolution value of about 715 ppb to 1,774 ppb in 2005. Methane is produced predominantly in agricultural production and also in burning fossil fuels, and the rapid increase in atmospheric methane is, like carbon dioxide, well beyond the natural range (320–790 ppm) of the past 650,000 years. Nitrous oxide is released by agricultural activities and is a greenhouse gas. Its concentration has increased in the atmosphere from a pre-industrial revolution level of 270 ppb to 319 ppb in 2005.

It has been estimated that the total increase in heating of the atmosphere due to anthropogenic increases in greenhouse gases since the start of the industrial revolution in 1750 is greater than other effects, and the rate of warming the planet is now experiencing is faster than any other experienced in the past 10,000 years. *Radiative forcing* is the net change in downward minus the upward irradiance at the tropopause,

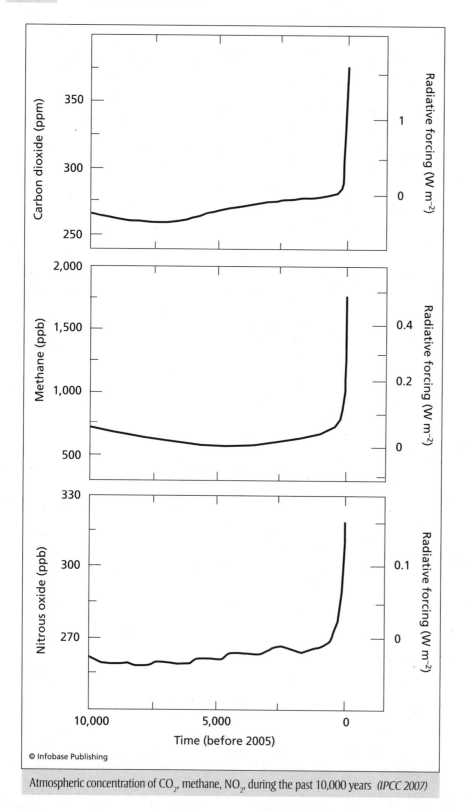

Atmospheric concentration of CO_2, methane, NO_2, during the past 10,000 years *(IPCC 2007)*

caused by a change in an external driver such as a change in greenhouse gas concentration. The radiative forcing caused by the change in CO_2 between 1995 and 2005 is estimated to be about 20 percent, the largest amount in the past 200 years. The way to counteract this is to enforce climate treaties such as the Kyoto Protocol, which calls for a reduction in CO_2 emissions through the installation of scrubbers and other cleansing technologies on factories and power plants and increasing the fuel efficiency of cars.

GLOBAL WARMING HOLES

Even though the global climate has been changing for billions of years by natural causes, it is clear that human activities are also presently changing the global climate, primarily through the introduction of greenhouse gases such as CO_2 into the atmosphere while cutting down tropical rain forests that act as sinks for the CO_2 and put oxygen back into the atmosphere. The time scale of observation of these human, or anthropogenic, changes is short, but the effect is clear, with a nearly one degree change in global temperature measured for the past few decades. The increase in temperature will lead to more water vapor in the atmosphere, and since water vapor is a greenhouse gas, this will lead to a further increase in temperature. Many computer-based climate models are attempting to predict how much global temperatures will rise as a consequence of anthropogenic input of gases to the atmosphere and what effects this temperature rise will have on melting of the ice sheets, sea level rise, and greenhouse temperature rise.

Climate changes are difficult to measure, partly because the instrumental and observational records go back only a couple of hundred years in Europe. From these records, global temperatures have risen about one degree since 1850, most notably between 1890 and 1940, and again since 1970. This variation, however, is small compared to some of the other variations induced by natural causes, and some scientists argue that it is difficult to separate anthropogenic effects from the background natural variations. Rainfall patterns have also changed in the past 50 years, with declining rainfall totals over low latitudes in the Northern Hemisphere, especially in the Sahel, which has experienced major droughts and famine, and in the Mediterranean, United States southwest, and Gobi Desert. However, high-latitude precipitation has increased in the same time period. These patterns all relate to a general warming and shifting of the global climate zones to the north.

Research by Dr. Zaito Pan's group at St. Louis University has shown that with global warming, some regions known as warming holes will actually become wetter and slightly colder than at present. In the United States, the central plains centered on the Missouri River Basin represent a warming hole, formed by the interaction between the convergence of water vapor leading to increased rainfall, accumulation of water in thick soils, and evaporation enhancing cooling. Other warming holes are predicted to grow in eastern China around Beijing and over the Amazon Basin of South America.

The increased precipitation is significant; for instance, a 21 percent increase in precipitation for the Missouri/Mississippi River basins is predicted in the central United States region, along with an alarming 51 percent increase in the amount of water flowing through the major rivers. River flood levels will be higher and floods will be more frequent and potentially devastating. The consequences of these climate changes are not appreciated and desperately need to be understood by the people who live in the region, developers, insurance underwriters, urban planners, politicians, and the federal government.

Some of the warming caused by increases in greenhouse gases may be counteracted by an increase in aerosols, small airborne solid or liquid particles, which may have a cooling effect. Aerosols include particles such as sulphate, organic carbon, black carbon, nitrates, and dust. As the climate warms, more and more dust is being picked up from regions that are undergoing increased aridness and desertification such as the fringes of the Gobi and Sahara Deserts. This dust gets emplaced high into the atmosphere where it may reside some time and may actually have a small cooling effect.

Cars emitting CO_2 during afternoon rush hour, San Diego Freeway, Los Angeles, California *(Shutterstock)*

Comparison of Short-term Climate Changes with the Medium-term Paleoclimate Record

It can be very difficult and complex to separate the effects of short-term human-induced climate changes from natural variations on longer-term time scales. The present day global warming is unusual for the climate record of the past 1,300 years, but has counterparts induced by natural causes about 125,000 years ago and in the older geological record. The

Power plant scrubber, to remove CO_2 from plant emissions *(Shutterstock)*

last time (125,000 years ago) climates warmed as significantly as the planet is now experiencing, loss of polar ice led to sea level rise of 13–20 feet (4–6 m), suggesting that the world's coastlines are in grave danger of moving inland to higher ground. Ice core data show that temperatures in Greenland were 4–7°F (3–5°C) hotter than present, a level that many models predict will be reached by the end of this century. The last 50 years appear to be the hottest in the past 1,300 years, but significant fluctuations have occurred.

The measured increases in anthropogenic greenhouse gases can more than account for the measured temperature rise of the surface of Earth in the past 50–100 years. The less-than-expected warming is probably related to lowering of the temperature by aerosols from volcanic eruptions and dust from desert environments. These measurements strongly suggest that the present-day global warming is being forced by the human-induced injection of greenhouse gases into the atmosphere, not by other long-term climate-forcing mechanisms that have controlled other global warming and cooling events in past geological times.

The measured surface warming is nearly global in scale, with the exception being Antarctica, which is sheltered from parts of the global atmosphere/ocean system. Climate models are consistent with the global warming being produced by anthropogenic causes. Many local variations exist, such as "warming holes," where local atmospheric effects are stronger than the global changes (see sidebar on page 51).

The global warming is also likely affecting wind patterns, the most extreme hot and cold nights, extratropical storm patterns, and causing an increase in heat waves. Effects are stronger in the Northern than in the Southern Hemisphere.

Sea Level Changes

Global sea levels are currently rising as a result of the melting of the Greenland and Antarctica ice sheets and thermal expansion of the world's ocean waters due to global warming. We are presently in an interglacial stage of an ice age, and sea levels have risen nearly 400 feet (130 m) since the last glacial maximum 20,000 years ago, and about six inches (15.25 cm) in the past 100 years. The rate of sea level rise seems to be accelerating and may presently be as much as an inch (2.5 cm) every 8–10 years. If all the ice on both ice sheets were to melt, global sea levels would rise by 230 feet (70 m), inundating most of the world's major cities and submerging large parts of the continents under shallow seas.

The coastal regions of the world are densely populated and are experiencing rapid population growth. Approximately 100 million people presently live within three feet (1 m) of the present day sea level. If sea level were to rise rapidly and significantly, the world would experience an economic and social disaster of a magnitude not yet experienced by the civilized world. Many areas would become permanently (on human time scales) flooded or subject to inundation by storms, *beach* erosion would be accelerated, and water tables would rise.

The Greenland and Antarctic ice sheets have some significant differences that cause them to respond differently to changes in air and water temperatures. The Antarctic ice sheet is about ten times as large as the Greenland ice sheet, and since it sits on the South Pole, Antarctica dominates its own climate. The surrounding ocean is cold even during summer, and much of Antarctica is a cold desert with low precipitation rates and high evaporation potential. Most meltwater in Antarctica seeps into underlying snow and simply refreezes, with little running off into the sea. Antarctica hosts several large ice shelves fed by glaciers moving at rates of up to a thousand feet (300 m) per year. Most ice loss in Antarctica is accomplished through *calving* and basal melting of the ice shelves, at rates of about 10–15 inches (25–38 cm) per year.

In contrast, Greenland's climate is influenced by warm North Atlantic currents and its proximity to other land masses. Climate data measured from ice cores taken from the top of the Greenland ice cap show that temperatures have varied significantly in cycles of years to decades. Greenland also experiences significant summer melting, abundant snowfall, has few ice shelves, and its glaciers move quickly at rates of up to miles (several km) per year. These fast-moving glaciers are able to drain a large amount of ice from Greenland in relatively short amounts of time.

The Greenland ice sheet is thinning rapidly along its edges, losing an average of 15–20 feet (4.5–6 m) in the past decade. In addition, tidewater glaciers and the small ice shelves in Greenland are melting an order of magnitude faster than the Antarctic ice sheets, with rates of melting between 25–65 feet (7.6–20 m) per year. About half of the ice lost from Greenland is through surface melting that runs off into the sea. The other half of ice loss is through calving of outlet glaciers and melting along the tidewater glaciers and ice shelf bases. If just the Greenland ice sheet melts, the water released will contribute another 23 feet (7 m) to sea level rise, to a level not seen since 125,000 years ago.

These differences between the Greenland and Antarctic ice sheets lead them to play different roles in global sea level rise. Greenland contributes more to the rapid short-term fluctuations in sea level, responding to short-term changes in climate. In contrast, most of the world's water available for raising sea level is locked up in the slowly changing Antarctic ice sheet. Antarctica contributes more to the gradual, long-term sea level rise.

Data released by the Intergovernmental Panel on Climate Change in 2007 points clearly to a cause of the recent melting of the glaciers. Most data suggests that the current melting is largely the result of the recent warming of the planet in the past 100 years through the effects of greenhouse warming. Greenhouse gases have been increasing at a rate of more than 0.2 percent per year, and global temperatures are rising accordingly. The most significant contributor to the greenhouse gas buildup is CO_2, produced mainly by the burning of fossil fuels. Other gases that contribute to greenhouse warming include carbon monoxide, nitrogen oxides, methane (CH_4), ozone (O_3) and chlorofluorocarbons. Methane is produced by gas from grazing animals and termites, whereas nitrogen oxides are increasing because of the increased use of fertilizers and automobiles, and the chlorofluorocarbons are increasing from release from aerosols and refrigerants. Together the greenhouse gases have the effect of allowing short-wavelength incoming solar radiation to penetrate the gas in the upper atmosphere, but trapping the solar radiation after it is re-emitted from Earth in a longer wavelength form. The trapped radiation causes the atmosphere to heat up, leading to greenhouse warming. Other factors also influence greenhouse warming and cooling, including the abundance of volcanic ash in the atmosphere and solar luminosity variations, as evidenced by sunspot variations.

Measuring global (also called *eustatic*) sea level rise and fall is difficult because many factors influence the relative height of the sea along any coastline. These vertical motions of continents are called *epeirogenic* movements, and may be related to plate tectonics, to rebound from being buried by glaciers, or to changes in the amount of heat added to the base of the continent by mantle convection. Continents may rise or sink vertically, causing apparent sea level change, but these sea level changes are relatively slow compared to changes induced by global warming and glacial melting. Slow, long-term sea level changes can also be induced by changes in the amount of seafloor volcanism associated with seafloor spreading. At some times in Earth history, seafloor spreading was particularly vigorous, and the increased volume of volcanoes and the mid-ocean ridge system caused global sea levels to rise.

Steady winds and currents can mass water against a particular coastline, causing a local and temporary sea level rise. Such a phenomenon is associated with the El Niño–Southern Oscillation (ENSO), causing sea levels to rise by 4–8 inches (10–20 cm) in the Australia-Asia region. When the warm water moves east in an ENSO event, sea levels may rise may 4–20 inches (10–50 cm) across much of the North and South American coastlines. Other atmospheric phenomena can also change sea level by centimeters to meters locally, on short time scales. Changes in atmospheric pressure, salinity of sea waters, coastal upwelling, onshore winds, and *storm surges* all cause short term fluctuations along segments of coastline. Global or local warming of waters can cause them to expand slightly, causing a local sea level rise. It is even thought that the extraction and use of ground water and its subsequent release into the sea might be causing sea level rise of about 0.05 inches (.13 cm) per year. Seasonal changes in river discharge can temporarily change sea levels along some coastlines, especially where winter cooling locks up large amounts of snow that melt in the spring.

It is clear that attempts to estimate eustatic sea level changes must be able to average out the numerous local and tectonic effects to arrive at a globally meaningful estimate of sea level change. Most coastlines seem to be dominated by local fluctuations that are larger in magnitude than any global sea level rise. Recently, satellite radar technology has been employed to precisely measure sea surface height and to document annual changes in sea level. Radar altimetry is able to map sea surface elevations to the sub-inch scale and to do this globally, providing an unprecedented level of understanding of sea surface topography. Satellite techniques support the concept that global sea levels are rising at about .1 inch per decade.

Conclusion

Even though Earth's climate has been changing between warm and cold periods for the past four and a half billion years, it is clear that humans have been rapidly increasing the amount of greenhouse gases in the atmosphere for the past 200 years. These gases, primarily carbon dioxide, have resulted in a new climate-forcing mechanism, whereby human or anthropogenic changes have forced the average global temperature to rise by nearly one degree in the past 200 years, and the temperature increase is continuing. The average land and sea surface temperatures have both increased, most notably over northern high latitudes, and the world's mountain glaciers and permafrost are receding and melting. Sea level is now rising at .12 inch per year (.31 cm/yr.), as a result of melting glaciers and thermal expansion of warming waters. Sea level is expected to continue to rise at least at this rate and may accelerate rapidly and rise by as much as 230 feet (70 m) if both the Greenland and Antarctic ice sheets were to melt. It is likely that the Greenland ice sheet will melt in the next few centuries, but the Antarctic ice sheet appears more stable and should survive longer. If only the Greenland ice sheet melts then sea levels will rise by an additional 23 feet (7 m), still placing the 100 million people who live within three feet (1 m) of present sea level in immediate danger.

4

Global Climate Changes That Lead to Droughts and Desert Formation

As the global climate warms, some climate belts, especially deserts, are expanding to higher latitudes, displacing once-fertile regions. Deserts are the driest places on Earth, by definition receiving less than one inch (2.5 cm) of rain per year. Most deserts are so dry that more moisture is able to evaporate than falls as precipitation. At present about 30 percent of the global landmass is desert, and the United States has about 10 percent desert areas. With changing global climate patterns and shifting climate zones, much more of the planet is in danger of becoming desert.

Most deserts are also hot, with the highest recorded temperature on record being 136° F in the Libyan Desert. With high temperatures, the evaporation rate is high, and in most cases able to evaporate more than the amount of precipitation that falls as rain. Many deserts are capable of evaporating 20 times the amount of rain that falls, and some places, like much of the northern Sahara, are capable of evaporating 200–300 times the amount of rain that falls in rare storms. Deserts are also famous for large variations in the daily temperature, sometimes changing as much as 50–70° between day and night (called a *diurnal cycle*). These large temperature variations are enough to shatter boulders in some cases. Deserts are dramatically windy places and are prone to sand and dust storms. The winds arise primarily because the heat of the day causes warm air to rise and expand, and other air must rush in to take its place. Airflow directions also shift frequently between day and night, in response to the large temperature difference between day and night, and between any nearby water bodies, which tend to stay at the same temperature between day and night.

There are many different types of deserts located in all different parts of the world. Some deserts are associated with patterns of global air circulation, and others form because they are in continental interiors far from any sources of moisture. Deserts may form on the "back" or *leeward* side of mountain ranges, where downwelling air is typically dry, or they may form along coasts where cold upwelling ocean currents lower the air temperature and lower its ability to hold moisture. Deserts may also form in polar regions, where extremely dry and cold air has the ability to evaporate (or sublimate) much more moisture than falls as snow in any given year. Parts of Antarctica such as the Dry Valleys have not had any significant ice or snow cover for thousands of years.

Deserts have a distinctive set of landforms and hazards associated with these landforms. The most famous desert landform is a sand *dune,* which is a mobile accumulation of sand that shifts in response to wind. Deserts are generally very windy places, and some of the hazards in deserts are associated with sand and dust carried by the wind. Dust eroded from deserts can be carried around the globe and is a significant factor in global climate, changing the reflectivity of the atmosphere and acting as nuclei for precipitation. Some sandstorms can be so fierce that they can remove the paint from cars or the skin from an unprotected person. Other hazards in deserts are associated with flash floods, debris flows, avalanches, extreme heat, and extreme fluctuations in temperature.

Droughts are different from deserts—a drought is a prolonged lack of rainfall in a region that typically gets more rainfall. If a desert normally gets a small amount of rainfall, and it still is getting little rainfall, then it is not experiencing a drought. In contrast, a different area that receives more rainfall than the desert may be experiencing a drought if it normally receives significantly more rainfall than it is at present. A drought-plagued area may become a desert if the drought is prolonged. Droughts are the most severe natural hazard in terms of their severity, area affected, loss of life and livelihood, social impact, and their long-term effects. Droughts can cause widespread famine, loss of vegetation, loss of life, and eventual death or mass migrations of entire populations.

Droughts may lead to conversion of previously productive lands to desert in a process called desertification. Desertification may occur if the land is stressed prior to or during the drought, typically from poor agricultural practices, overuse of ground and surface water resources, and overpopulation. Global climate goes through several different variations that can cause belts of aridity to shift back and forth with time. The Sahel region of Africa has experienced some of the more severe droughts in recent times. The Middle East and parts of the desert Southwest of the United Sates are overpopulated and the environment is stressed. If major droughts occur in these regions, major famines could result and the land may be permanently desertified.

Processes That Lead to the Formation of Deserts

More than 35 percent of the land area on the planet is arid or semi-arid, and these deserts form a distinctive pattern on the globe that reveals clues about how they form. There are six main categories of desert based on their geographic location with respect to continental margins, oceans, and mountains.

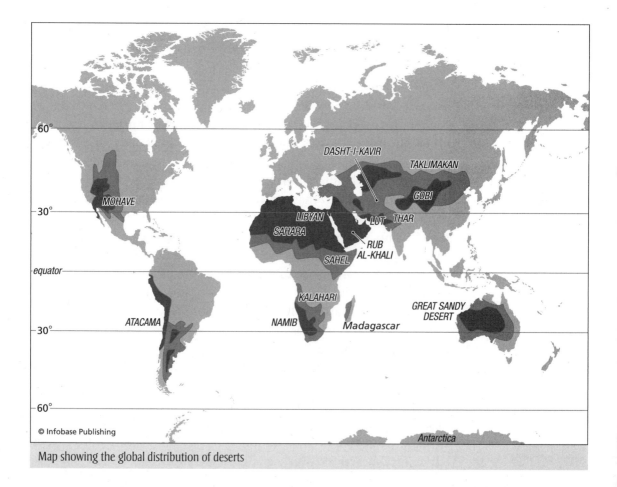

Map showing the global distribution of deserts

TRADE WIND OR HADLEY CELL DESERTS

Many of the world's largest and driest deserts are located in two belts between 15° and 30° north and south latitude. Included in this group of deserts are the Sahara, the world's largest desert, and the Libyan Desert of North Africa. Other members of this group include the Syrian Desert, Rub a'Khali (Empty Quarter) and Great Sand Desert of Arabia; the Dasht-i-Kavir, Lut, and Sind of Southwest Asia; the Thar Desert of Pakistan; and the Mojave and Sonoran Deserts of the United States (although the latter are also in the *rain shadows* of coastal mountain ranges). In the Southern Hemisphere, deserts that fall into this group include Kalahari Desert of Africa and the Great Sandy Desert of Australia, and this effect contributes to the formation of the Atacama Desert in South America, the world's driest place.

The location of these deserts is controlled by a large-scale atmospheric circulation pattern that forms Hadley cells, driven by energy from the Sun. The Sun heats equatorial regions more than high-latitude areas, which causes large-scale atmospheric upwelling near the equator. This air rises, and as it rises it becomes less dense and can hold less moisture which helps form large thunderstorms in equatorial areas. This drier air then moves away from the equator at high altitudes, cooling and drying more as it does, until it eventually forms two circumglobal downwelling belts between 15–30° N and S latitude. This cold downwelling air is dry and has the ability to hold much more water than it has brought with it on its circuit from the equator. These belts of circulating air are known as Hadley Cells and are responsible for the formation of many of the world's largest, driest deserts. As this air completes its circuit back to the equator, it forms dry winds that heat up as they move toward the equator. The dry winds dissipate existing cloud cover and allow more sunlight to reach the surface, which then warms these deserts even more.

Deserts formed by global circulation patterns are particularly sensitive to changes in global climate, and seemingly small changes in the global circulation may lead to catastrophic expansion or contraction of some of the world's largest deserts. For instance, the sub-Saharan Sahel has experienced several episodes of expansion and contraction of the Sahara, displacing or killing millions of people in this vicious cycle. When deserts expand, croplands are dried up, and livestock and people can not find enough water to survive. Desert expansion is the underlying cause of some of the world's most severe famines.

CONTINENTAL INTERIOR/MIDLATITUDE DESERTS

Some places on Earth are so far from ocean moisture sources that by the time weather systems reach them, most of the moisture they carry has already fallen. This effect is worsened if the weather systems have to rise over mountains or plateaus to reach these areas, because cloud

IS THERE A DROUGHT IN LAS VEGAS?

Much of the desert Southwest region of the United States was settled in the past century following a century of historically high rainfall. Towns and cities grew, and the Bureau of Land Management diverted water from melting snows, rivers, and underground *aquifers* to meet the needs of growing cities. Some of the country's largest and newest cities, including Phoenix, Tucson, Denver, Las Vegas, Los Angeles, San Diego, and Albuquerque, have grown out of the desert using water from the Colorado River system. Even though the temperatures can be high, the air is good, and many people have chosen to move to these regions to escape crowded, polluted, or allergen-rich cities and air elsewhere. The surge in population has been met with increases in the water diverted to these cities, and fountains, swimming pools, resorts, golf courses, and green lawns have sprung up all over. In general the life can be comfortable.

In the past decade the water seems to be diminishing. Lake Powell in Arizona has shrunk to half its capacity, and the Colorado River flow shrunk to a quarter of its typical rates. The Colorado River is used to supply 30 million people with water and irrigates four million acres of fertile farmland, producing billions of dollars worth of crops. The massive waterworks systems across seven states in the southwest were all built using river flow data for the Colorado River based on 20th century flow records. Now, studies of the ancient climate history in the region going back thousands of years indicate that the 20th century may have been one of the wettest on record for the region. The Hoover Dam, the California aqueduct, and cities across the region were all built during this high flow stage of the Colorado River, and water budgets for the region were calculated assuming these flows would continue. Now, precipitation is decreasing, and the historical records show that the region regularly experiences droughts where the flow decreases to 80 percent and even 50 percent of the 20th century values used for building the civilization in the desert Southwest. Now that more than 80 percent of the water from the river is used for human consumption, droughts of this magnitude have severe implications for any community, and the water wars of the Southwest may eventually start again. Historical records show that past civilizations such as the Anasazi in the region disappeared at the end of the 13th century during a similar drought period, and similar trends are expected by climate modelers for the future in the region.

Climate change models released by the National Ocean and Atmospheric Administration show that the flow of the Colorado River may decrease to half of its 20th century values by the middle of this century and that these lower flow values will persist into the foreseeable future. The region is already experiencing rapid changes, with wildfires burning huge tracts of vegetation and occasional storms initiating *mudflows* and other desert processes. Climate models predict a likely descent of the region into dust bowl conditions and that these changes have already begun. The region saw many mega-droughts in medieval times and throughout history, and states of the region need to prepare for the likelihood of many years of water shortage and increasing drought conditions.

systems typically lose moisture as they rise over mountains. These remote areas therefore have little chance of receiving significant rainfalls. The most significant desert in this category is the Taklimakan-Gobi region of China, resting south of the Mongolian steppe on the Alashan plateau, and the Karakum of western Asia. The Gobi is the world's northernmost large desert, and it is characterized by 1,000-foot-high sand dunes made of coarser than normal sand and gravel, built up layer by layer by material moved and deposited by the wind. It is a desolate region, conquered successively by Genghis Khan, warriors of the Ming dynasty, then the People's Army of China. The sands are still

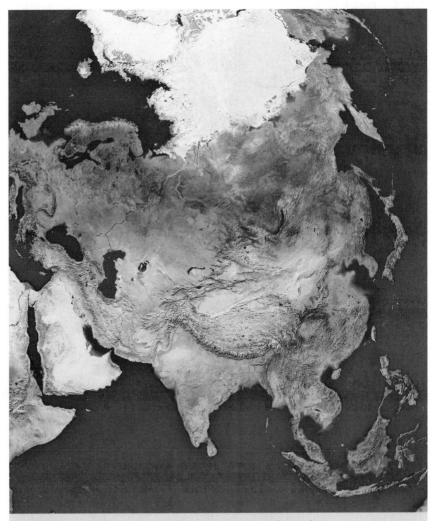

Satellite image of Asia showing the prominent and expanding Gobi Desert
(*Photo Researchers*)

littered with remains of many of these battles, such as the abandoned city of Khara Khoto. In 1372, Ming dynasty warriors conquered this walled city by cutting off its water supply consisting of the Black River, making a blockade and siege of the city, then massacring all remaining people in the city.

RAINSHADOW DESERTS

A third type of desert is found on the leeward (or back) side of some large mountain ranges, such as the sub-Andean Patagonian Gran Chaco and Pampas of Argentina, Paraguay, and Bolivia. A similar effect is partly responsible for the formation of the Mojave and Sonoran Deserts of the United States (although these are also in the belt of global 15–30° latitude downwelling dry air). These deserts form because as moist air masses move toward the mountain ranges they must rise to move over the ranges. As the air rises it cools, and cold air can hold less moisture than warm air. The clouds thus drop much of their moisture on the *windward* side of the mountains, explaining why places like the western Cascades and western Sierras of the United States are extremely wet, as are the western Andes in Peru. However the eastern lee sides (or back sides) of these mountains are extremely dry. The reason for this is that as the air rose over the fronts or windward sides of the mountains, it dropped its moisture as it rose. As the same air descends on the lee side of the mountains it

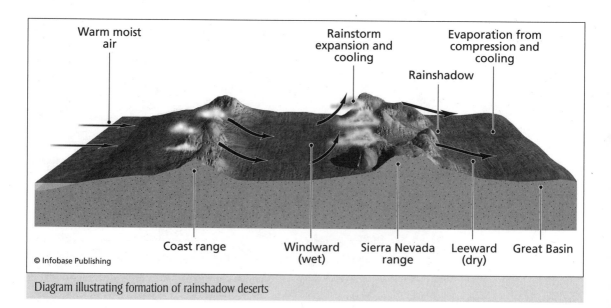

© Infobase Publishing

Diagram illustrating formation of rainshadow deserts

gets warmer, and is able to hold more moisture than it has left in the clouds. The result it that the air is dry and it rarely rains. This explains why places like the eastern sub-Andean region of South America and the Sonoran and Mojave Deserts of the western United States are extremely dry.

Rainshadow deserts tend to be mountainous because of the way they form, and they are associated with a number of mass-wasting hazards such as landslides, debris flows, and avalanches. Occasional rain storms that make it over the blocking mountain ranges can drop moisture in the highlands, leading to flash floods coming out of mountain canyons into the plains or intermountain basins on the lee side of the mountains.

COASTAL DESERTS

There are some deserts that are located along coastlines, where intuition would seem to indicate that moisture should be plentiful. However, the driest place on Earth is the Atacama Desert, located along the coast of Peru and Chile. The Namib Desert of southern Africa is another coastal desert, which is known legendarily as the Skeleton Coast, because it is so dry that many of the large animals that roam out of the more humid interior climate zones in search of food perish there, leaving their bones sticking out of the blowing sands. The waters off the Skeleton Coast are also known as particularly treacherous, with strong currents and rogue waves leading to many shipwrecks.

These coastal deserts form adjacent to such large bodies of water where ocean currents place cold upwelling water from the deep ocean next to the coast, which cools the atmosphere. The effect is similar to rainshadow deserts, where cold air can hold less moisture, and the result is no rain.

MONSOON DESERTS

In some places on the planet, seasonal variations in wind systems bring alternating dry and wet seasons. The Indian Ocean is famous for its monsoonal rains in the summer as the southeast trade winds bring moist air on shore. However, as the moisture moves across India it loses moisture and must rise to cross the Aravalli Mountain Range. The Thar Desert of Pakistan and the Rajasthan Desert of India are located on the back or lee side of these mountains and do not generally receive this seasonal moisture.

POLAR DESERTS

A final class of deserts is the polar desert, found principally in the Dry Valleys and other parts of Antarctica, parts of Greenland, northern Canada, and Nunavut. Approximately 3 million square miles (7,770,000 km²) on Earth consists of polar desert environments. In these places, cold downwelling air lacks moisture, and the air is so dry that the evaporation potential is much greater than the precipitation. Temperatures do not exceed 50°F (10°C) in the warmest months, and precipitation is less than one inch per year. There are places in the Dry Valleys of Antarctica that have not been covered in ice for thousands of years.

Polar deserts are generally not covered in sand dunes, but are marked by gravel plains or barren bedrock. Hazards to travelers in polar deserts include the effects of extreme cold such as hypothermia, frostbite, and dehydration. Polar deserts may also have landforms shaped by frost wedging, where alternating freeze-thaw cycles allow small amounts of water to seep into cracks and other openings in rocks. When the water freezes it expands, pushing large blocks of rock away from the main mountain mass. In polar deserts and other regions affected by frost wedging large *talus* slopes may form adjacent to mountain fronts, and these are prone to frequent rock falls from frost wedging.

Some desert areas seem out of place; for instance, a large area of sand dunes in north-central Alaska looks like it belongs in the Sahara of North Africa. Many deserts like this are actually paleo-deserts, remnants of past dry climates, that have not yet converted into more fertile land. The sand dune fields in central Alaska are surrounded by pine forest and tundra, gradually replacing the old desert environment.

Desert Landforms

Desert landforms are some of the most beautiful on Earth, often presenting bizarre sculpted mountains, steep walled canyons, and regional gravel plains. They can also be some of the most hazardous landscapes on the planet. The *regolith* in deserts is thin, discontinuous, and much coarser-grained than in moist regions and is produced predominantly by mechanical weathering. Chemical weathering is of only minor importance, because of the rare moisture. Also, the coarse size of particles produced by mechanical weathering produces steep slopes, eroded from steep cliffs and escarpments.

Much of the regolith that sits in deserts is coated with a dark coating of manganese and iron oxides, known as desert varnish, produced by a combination of microorganism activity and chemical reactions with fine manganese dust that settles from the wind.

DESERT DRAINAGE SYSTEMS

Most streams in deserts evaporate before they reach the sea. Most are dry for long periods of time, and subject to *flash floods* during brief but intense rains. These flash floods transport most of the sediment in deserts and form fan-shaped deposits of sand, gravel, and boulders found at the bases of many mountains in desert regions. These flash floods also erode deep steep-walled canyons through the upstream mountain regions, which is the source of the boulders and cobbles found on the mountain fronts. Intermountain areas in deserts typically have finer-grained material, deposited by slower moving currents that represent the waning stages of floods as they expand into open areas between mountains after they escape out of mountain canyons.

Flash floods can be particularly hazardous in desert environments, especially when the floods are the result of distant rains. More people die in deserts from drowning in flash floods than die from thirst or dehydration. In many cases rain in far away mountains may occur, without people in downstream areas even aware that it is raining upstream. Rain in deserts is typically a brief but intense thunderstorm, which can drop a couple of inches (> 5 cm) of rain in a short time. The water may then quickly

Desert mountain wadi, Northern Oman Hajar Mountains *(T. Kusky)*

move downstream as a wall of water in mountain canyons, sweeping away all loose material in its path. Any people or vehicles caught in such a flood are likely to be lost, swept away by the swiftly moving torrent.

Dry lake beds in low-lying flat areas, which may have water in them only once every few years, characterize many deserts. These are known as *playas*, or hardpans, and they typically have deposits of white salts, which formed when water from storms evaporated leaving the lakes dry. There are more than 100 *playas* in the American Southwest, including Lake Bonneville, which formed during the last ice age and now covers parts of Utah, Nevada, and Idaho. When there is water in these basins, they are known as playa lakes. Playas are very flat surfaces that make excellent race tracks and runways. The U.S. space shuttles commonly land on Rogers Lake playa at Edwards Air Force Base in California.

Alluvial fans are coarse-grained deposits of alluvium that accumulate at the fronts of mountain canyons. Alluvial fans are very common in deserts, where they are composed of both alluvium and debris flow deposits. Alluvial fans are quite important for people in deserts, because they are porous and permeable and they contain large deposits of *groundwater*. In many places, alluvial fans so dominate the land surface that they form a *bajada* (or slope) along the base of the mountain range, formed by fans that have coalesced to form a continuous broad alluvial apron.

Pediments represent different kinds of desert surfaces. They are surfaces sloping away from the base of a highland and covered by a thin or discontinuous layer of alluvium and rock fragments. These are erosional features, formed by running water, and are typically cut by shallow channels. Pediments grow as mountains are eroded.

Inselbergs are steep-sided mountains or ridges that rise abruptly out of adjacent monotonously flat plains in deserts. Ayres Rock in central Australia is perhaps the world's best known inselberg. These are produced by differential erosion, leaving behind as a mountain rocks that for some reason are more resistant to erosion.

Wind in Deserts

Wind plays a significant role in the evolution of desert landscapes. Wind erodes in two basic ways. *Deflation* is a process whereby wind picks up and removes material from an area, resulting in a reduction in the land surface. The process is akin to deflating a balloon below the surface, hence its name. *Abrasion* is a different process that occurs when particles of sand and other sizes are blown by the wind and impact each

Man in donkey cart in dust storm in Sahara Desert in Algeria *(Corbis)*

other. Exposed surfaces in deserts are subjected to frequent abrasion, which is similar to sandblasting.

Yardangs are elongate streamlined wind-eroded ridges, which resemble an overturned ship's hull sticking out of the water. These unusual features are formed by abrasion, by the long-term sandblasting along specific corridors. The sandblasting leaves erosionally resistant ridges, but removes the softer material which itself will contribute to sandblasting in the downwind direction, and eventually contribute to the formation of sand, silt, and dust deposits.

Deflation is important on a large scale in places where there is no vegetation, and in some places the wind has excavated large basins known as deflation basins. Deflation basins are common in the United States from Texas to Canada as elongate (several miles/kilometers long) depressions, typically only 3–10 feet (0.9–3 m) deep. However, in some places like in the Sahara, deflation basins may be as much as several hundred feet deep.

Deflation by wind can move only small particles away from the source, since the size of the particle that can be lifted is limited by the strength of the wind, which rarely exceeds a few tens of miles per hour (~ 50 km/h). Deflation therefore leaves boulders, cobbles and other large particles behind. These get concentrated on the surface of deflation basins and other surfaces in deserts, leaving a surface concentrated in boulders known as desert pavement.

Desert pavements represent a long-term stable desert surface, and they are not particularly hazardous. However, when the desert pavement is broken, for instance, by being driven across, the coarse cobbles and pebbles get pushed beneath the surface and the underlying sands get exposed to wind action again. Driving across a desert pavement can raise a considerable amount of sand and dust, and if many vehicles drive across the surface then it can be destroyed and the whole surface becomes active.

A very striking large-scale example of this process was provided by events in the Gulf War of 1991. After Iraq invaded Kuwait in 1990, U.S. and Allied Forces massed hundreds of thousands of troops on the Saudi Arabian side of the border with Iraq and Kuwait, and eventually mounted a multi-pronged counterattack on Kuwait City that led to its liberation. Several of the prongs circled far to the north then turned around and came back south to Kuwait City. These prongs took many thousands of heavy tanks, artillery, and vehicles across a region of stable desert pavement, and the weight of these military vehicles destroyed the pavement in order to free Kuwait. Since the liberation, the steady winds from the northwest have continued, and this area that was once stable desert pavement and stable dune surfaces (covered with desert pavement and minor vegetation) has been remobilized. Large sand dunes have formed from the sand previously trapped under the pavement. Other dunes that were stable have been reactivated. Now, the Kuwait City residents are bracing for what they call the second invasion of Kuwait, but this time the invading force is sand and dust, not a foreign army.

Several things have been considered to try to stabilize the newly-migrating dunes. One consideration is to try to re-establish the desert pavement by spreading cobbles across the surface, but this is unrealistic because of the large area involved. Another proposition, being tested, is to spray petroleum on the migrating dunes to effectively create a black-top or tarred surface that would be stable in the wind. This is feasible in oil-rich Kuwait, but not particularly environmentally friendly.

In China's Gobi and Taklimakan Deserts, a different technique to stabilize dunes has proven rather successful. Bales of hay are initially placed in a grid pattern near the base of the windward side of dunes, which decreases the velocity of the air flowing over the dune and reduces the transportation of sand grains over the slip surface. Drought-resistant vegetation is planted between the several-foot-wide grid of hay bales, and then when the dune is more stabilized, vegetation is planted along the dune crest. China is applying this technique across much of the Gobi and Taklimakan Deserts, protecting railways and roads. In northeastern China, this technique is being applied in an attempt to reclaim some lands that became desert through human activity, and they are constructing a 5,700-mile- (9,173.3-km-) long line of hay bales and drought-resistant vegetation. China is said to be building a new "Green Wall" which will be longer than the famous Great Wall of China and it is hoped will prove more effective at keeping out invading forces (in this case, sand) from Mongolia.

Windblown Sand and Dust

Most people think of deserts as areas with lots of big sand dunes and continual swirling winds of dust storms. Really, dunes and dust storms

Sand dunes moving into populated agricultural area, Singing Mountain in Gobi Desert, China *(Photo Researchers)*

are not as common as depicted in popular movies, and rocky deserts are more common than sandy deserts. For instance, only about 20 percent of the Sahara Desert is covered by sand, and the rest is covered by rocky, pebbly, or gravel surfaces. However, sand dunes are locally very important in deserts, and wind is one of the most important processes in shaping deserts worldwide. Shifting sands are one of the most severe geologic hazards of deserts. In many deserts and desert border areas, the sands are moving into inhabited areas, covering farmlands, villages, and other useful land with thick accumulations of sand. This is a global problem, as deserts are currently expanding worldwide. The Desert Research Institute in China has recently estimated that in China alone, 950 square miles (2,460 km²) are encroached on by migrating sand dunes from the Gobi Desert each year, costing the country 6.7 billion dollars per year and affecting the lives of 400 million people.

Wind moves sand by *saltation*, in arced paths, in a series of bounces or jumps. The surface of dunes on beaches or deserts is typically covered by a thin moving layer of sand particles that are bouncing and rolling along the surface in this process of saltation.

Wind typically sorts different sizes of sedimentary particles, forming elongate small ridges known as sand ripples, very similar to ripples found in streams. Sand dunes are larger than ripples, up to 1,500 feet (ca. 450 m) high, made of mounds or ridges of sand deposited by wind.

These may form where an obstacle distorts or obstructs the flow of air, or they may move freely across much of a desert surface. Dunes have many different forms, but all are asymmetrical. They have a gentle slope that faces into the wind and a steep face that faces away from the wind. Sand particles move by saltation up the windward side, and fall out near the top where the pocket of low-velocity air can not hold the sand anymore. The sand avalanches, or slips down, the leeward slope, known as the slip face. This keeps the slope at the angle of repose, 30–34°. The asymmetry of old dunes is used to tell the directions ancient winds blew.

The steady movement of sand from one side of the dune to the other causes the whole dune to migrate slowly downwind, typically about 80–100 feet (28–30 m) per year, burying houses, farmlands, temples, and towns. Rates of dune migration of up to 350 feet (107 m) per year have been measured in the Western Desert of Egypt and the Ningxia Province of China.

A combination of many different factors leads to the formation of very different types of dunes, each with a distinctive shape, potential for movement, and hazards. The main variables that determine a dune's shape are the amount of sand that is available for transportation, the strength (and directional uniformity) of the wind, and the amount of vegetation that covers the surface. If there is a lot of vegetation and little wind, no dunes will form. In contrast, if there is very little vegetation, a lot of sand, and moderate wind strength (conditions that might be found on a beach), then a group of dunes known as transverse dunes forms, with the dune crests aligned at right angles to the dominant wind.

Barchan dunes have crescent-shapes and have horns pointing downwind and form on flat deserts with steady winds and a limited sand supply. Parabolic dunes have a U-shape with the U facing upwind. These form where there is significant vegetation that pins the tails of migrating transverse dunes, with the dune being warped into a wide U-shape. These dunes look broadly similar to barchans, except the tails point in the opposite direction. They can be distinguished because in both cases, the steep side of the dune points away from the dominant winds direction. Linear dunes are long, straight ridge-shaped dunes elongate parallel to the wind direction. These occur in deserts with little sand supply and strong, slightly variable winds, and they are elongate

(Opposite) Sand dune types and classification based on relative strength of wind, sand supply, and vegetation. A, barchan dunes; B, transverse dunes; C, barchanoid dunes; D, longitudinal dunes; E, parabolic dunes; F, star dunes

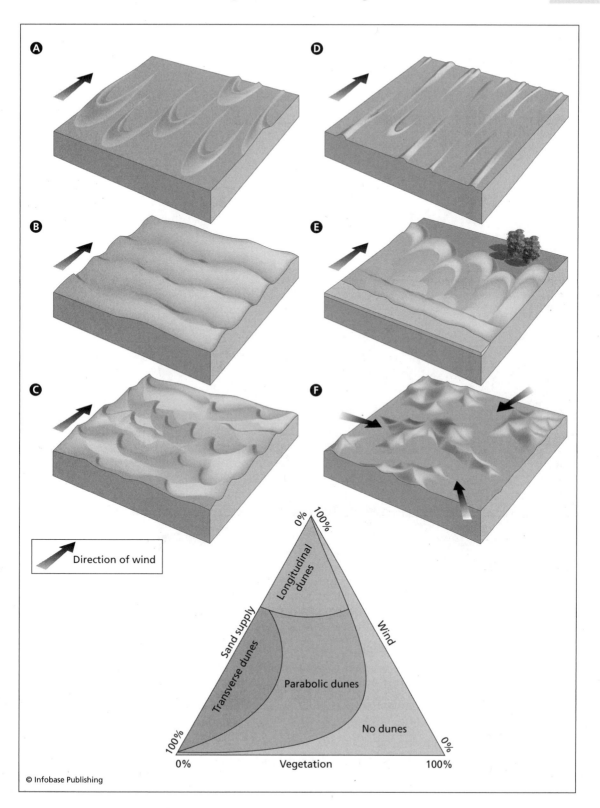

Direction of wind

Dust storm on Badaling Great Wall near Beijing, March 20, 2002 *(AP)*

parallel to the wind direction. Star dunes form isolated or irregular hills formed where the wind directions are irregular.

Strong winds that blow across desert regions sometimes pick up dust made of silt and clay particles and transport it thousands of kilometers from its source. For instance, dust from China is found in Hawaii, and the Sahara Desert commonly drops dust in Europe. This dust is a nuisance, has a significant influence on global climate, and has at times, as in the dust bowl days of the 1930s, been known to nearly block out the Sun.

Loess is a name for silt and clay deposited by wind. It forms a uniform blanket that covers hills and valleys at many altitudes, which distinguishes it from deposits of streams. In Shaanxi Province, China, an earthquake that killed 830,000 people in 1556 had such a high death toll in part because the people in the region built their homes out of loess. The loess formed an easily excavated material that hundreds of thousands of villagers cut homes into, essentially living in caves. When the earthquake struck, the loess proved to be a poor building material and large-scale collapse of the fine-grained loess was directly responsible for most of the high death toll.

Recently, it has been recognized that wind-blown dust contributes significantly to global climate. Dust storms that come out of the Sahara can be carried around the world and can partially block out some of the Sun's radiation. The dust particles may also act as small nuclei for raindrops to form around, perhaps acting as a natural cloud-seeding phenomenon. One interesting point to ponder is that as global warming increases global temperatures, the amount and intensity of storms increase, and some of the world's deserts expand. Dust storms may serve to counter this effect, reduce global temperatures, and increase precipitation.

Conclusion

Deserts are places that receive less than one inch (2.5 cm) of rainfall per year, with some deserts being capable of evaporating hundreds of times more precipitation than actually falls. Deserts form in a variety of environments, including locations in continental interiors that are far from sources of water, along coastlines where cold upwelling water reduces the capacity of the air to hold water, and in rainshadows where moist air that moves up one side of a mountain drops its moisture on that side and descends as a dry air mass. Some of the world's largest deserts form between 15 and 30° latitude by cold descending air masses formed by global air circulation patterns. These deserts, such as the Sahara, are expanding as the global climate warms and represent a significant threat as drought and famine spread across areas such as the Sahel that border these regions. Drought and famine in expanding deserts represent one of the most serious threats to large populations in affected areas and have the potential to cause the deaths and suffering of millions of people as global climate warms and deserts expand. Other hazards from deserts include wind-blown sand and dust that can circle the globe and more local hazards such as drifting sand and flash floods.

5

Examples of Expanding Deserts and Drought Disasters

Global climate change is causing many areas on the planet that were previously experiencing temperate climates to suffer drought conditions. Drought is very different from normal desert processes. A drought is a prolonged reduction in the amount of rainfall for a region. It is one of the slowest of all major natural disasters to affect people, but it is also among the most severe, causing more deaths, famine, and displacement than most other more spectacular disasters.

Drought often presages the expansion of desert environments, and regions like Africa's sub-Saharan Sahel have experienced periods of drought and desert expansion and contraction several times in the past few tens of thousands of years. At present much of the Sahara is expanding southward, and peoples of the Sahel have suffered immensely.

Droughts typically begin imperceptibly, with seasonal rains often not appearing on schedule. Farmers and herdsmen may be waiting for the rains to water their freshly planted fields and to water their flocks, but the rains do not appear. Local water sources such as streams, rivers, and springs may begin to dry up until eventually, only deep wells are able to extract water out of groundwater aquifers. This is typically not enough to sustain crops and livestock, so they begin to be slaughtered or die of starvation and dehydration. Crops do not grow, and natural vegetation begins to dry up and die. Brush fires often come next, wiping away the dry brush. Soon people start to become weak, and they can not manage to walk out of the affected areas, so they stay, and the

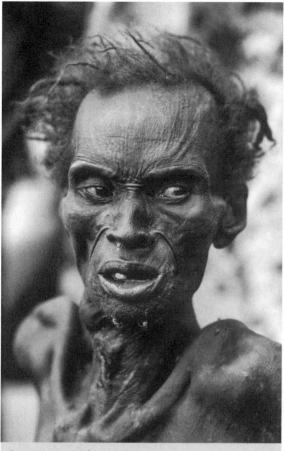

Starving man in Thiet, Sudan *(Getty)*

weak, elderly, and young of the population may die off. Famine and disease may follow, killing even more people.

Drought Caused by Changes in Global Atmospheric Circulation

Droughts have many different causes. Global oceanic and atmospheric circulation patterns undergo frequent shifts that affect large parts of the globe, particularly those arid and semi-arid parts affected by Hadley Cell circulation. One of the better known variations in global circulation is known as the El Niño–Southern Oscillation. Fluctuations in global circulation can account for natural disasters, including the Dust Bowl days of the 1930s in the U.S. plains states. Similar global climate fluctuations may explain the drought, famine, and desertification of parts of the Sahel and the great famines of Ethiopia and Sudan in the 1970s, 1980s, and mid-2000s. Much of Africa, including the Sahel region, has become increasingly dry and desert-like over the past 100 years or more, and any attempts to restart agriculture and repopulate regions evacuated during previous famines in this region may be fruitless and lead to further loss of life.

Hadley Cells are the name given to the globe-encircling belts of air that rise along the equator, dropping moisture as they rise in the tropics. As the air moves away from the equator, it cools and becomes drier, then descends at 15–30° N and S latitude, where it either returns to the equator or moves poleward. The locations of the Hadley Cells move north and south annually, in response to the changing apparent seasonal movement of the Sun. High-pressure systems form where the air descends, and stable clear skies and intense evaporation characterize these because the air is so dry. Another pair of major global circulation belts is formed as air cools at the poles and spreads toward the equator. Cold polar fronts form where the polar air mass meets the warmer air that has circulated around the Hadley Cell from the tropics. In the belts between the polar front and the Hadley Cells, strong westerly winds develop. The position of the polar front and extent of the west-moving wind is controlled by the position of the polar jet stream (formed in the upper troposphere), which is partly fixed in place in the Northern Hemisphere by the high Tibetan Plateau and the Rocky Mountains. Dips and bends in the jet stream path are known as Rossby Waves, and these partly determine the location of high- and low-pressure systems. These Rossby Waves tend to be semi-stable in different seasons, and have predictable patterns for summer and winter. If the pattern of Rossby Waves in the jet stream changes significantly for a season or longer, it may cause storm systems to track to different locations than normal, causing local droughts or floods. Changes to this global circulation may also change the locations of regional downwelling cold dry air. This can cause long-term drought and desertification. Such changes may persist for periods of several weeks, months, or years and may explain several of the severe droughts that have affected Asia, Africa, North America, and elsewhere.

The El Niño–Southern Oscillation air circulation phenomenon can also have strong influences on the locations and strength of drought conditions and desertification of stressed lands. Hadley Cells migrate north and south with summer and winter, shifting the locations of the most intense heating. The switching between ENSO, La Niña, and normal ocean-atmospheric circulation patterns has profound effects on global climate and the migration of different climate belts on yearly to decadal time scales and is thought to account for about a third of all the variability in global rainfall. ENSO events may cause flooding in the western Andes and southern California and a lack of rainfall in other parts of South America including Venezuela, northeastern Brazil, and southern Peru. Analysis of past climate and circulation data has suggested the El Niño–Southern Oscillation was at least partly to blame for the dust bowl days of the 1930s across much of the central and western United States.

Drought and Desertification in the Sahel and Sub-Saharan Africa

The Sahel region offers one of the world's most tragic examples of how poorly managed agricultural practices, politics, and religious differences, when mixed with long term drought conditions, can lead to disaster and permanent desertification. A similar lesson is found in the Rajputana desert of India, one of the cradles of civilization that has become desert because of poor land use coupled with natural drought cycles.

CHINA'S EFFORT TO HALT EXPANSION OF THE GOBI DESERT

China's agriculture, economy, industry, population, and personal wealth have been growing at a remarkable rate. From 1950 to 1998 the grain production in China grew from 90 million tons to 392 million tons, fueling this growth. However, some trends in climate are starting to threaten this growth, and the Chinese government is making huge efforts to counteract these potentially negative trends. After 2003, the grain harvest began declining because of water shortages in the northern and western parts of the country, where the wheat crops have been suffering drought and expansion of the Gobi Desert. The loss of arable land is due to expansion of the desert as well as loss of irrigation water and the changing of farm lands into other uses. A mass migration of the people of China from rural farmlands in the west and center of the country to the relatively wealthy east has also resulted in a loss of farm labor, further decreasing the crop yields.

China has been actively seeking ways to slow the expansion of the Gobi Desert, estimated to be growing at 4,000 square miles (10,360 km^2) per year. Massive tree planting campaigns have been mounted, trying to slow the shifting of the sands into existing farm lands. Diversions of water from the humid south to the north of the country are underway, representing some of the most massive waterworks projects in the world. Groundwater resources are being sought for irrigation, and the Chinese government is investing billions of dollars into trying to halt the expansion of the desert, making it one of the nation's top priorities in 2007. Still, the trends in loss of farmland and migration of farm workers to eastern industrial cities means that China needs to make the transition from a grain-producing and exporting country to a grain importer. The scale of the expected grain imports is huge, as the 1.4 billion people in China will need to turn to the United States, the world's largest grain exporter, to purchase food. This will drive up the price of food in the United States but bring the two countries economically much closer.

The Climate Change 2007 report issued by the Intergovernmental Panel on Climate Change has some predictions for China. With rising temperatures, China has been experiencing more warming in the winter than the summer and is seeing a more rapid increase in the minimum temperatures, while the daily maximum temperatures remain about the same. The annual rains are decreasing in northeast and northern China, while increasing in westernmost China, along the Changjiang River, and along the southeast coast. Short duration heat waves have been increasing in frequency, and intense rains and floods are becoming more frequent in western and southern China, especially along the Changjiang River, while summer rains are becoming more steady in eastern China. Northern China is experiencing a decrease in intense rainfall events. The Gobi Desert is continuing to expand toward the Beijing area, including Hebei and Shanxi Provinces, Inner Mongolia, and northern China, with frequent dust storms. The southeastern coastal region of China is seeing a strong increase in the number of typhoons that affect the region, many with extreme storm surges that move into coastal areas. Availability of fresh water resources across the region is expected to become scarcer, as these climate trends continue and the population continues to grow.

Sahel means boundary in Arabic, and the Sahel forms the southern boundary of the world's largest desert, the Sahara. The Sahel is situated mostly between 14° and 18° N latitude, characterized by scrubby grasslands, getting on average between 14–23 inches (35.6–58.4 cm) of rain per year. It is home to about 25 million people, most of whom are nomadic herders and subsistence farmers. In the summer months of June and July, heating normally causes air to rise and this is replaced by moist air from the Atlantic, which brings the annual rainfall. The Sahel has experienced the ravages of many fluctuations in climate change events. In 1968, the normal northward movement of the wet intertropical convergence zone stopped during an ENSO event, and further climatic changes in the 1970s led to only about half of the normal rain falling up until 1975. With additional lack of moisture brought on by complications from the temperature cycles of the northern and southern oceans becoming out of synchronicity at this time, the region suffered long-term drought and permanent desertification.

As the rains continued to fail to come and the air masses continued to evaporate surface water, the soil moisture was drastically reduced, which further reduced evaporation and cloud cover. The vegetation soon died off, and the soils became dry and hot and near-surface temperatures were further increased. Soon, the plants were gone, the soils were exposed to the wind, and the region became plagued with blowing dust and sand. Approximately 200,000 people died, and 12 million head of livestock perished. Parts of the region were altered to desert, with little chance of returning to the previous state.

The desertification of the Sahel was enhanced by the agricultural practices of the people of the region. Nomadic and marginal agriculture was strongly dependent on the monsoon, and when the rains did not come for several years, the natural and planted crops died. Many of the remaining plants were used as fuel for fires to offset the cost of fuel. This practice greatly accelerated the desertification process. The Sahara is now thought to be overtaking the Sahel by migrating southward at approximately three miles (5 km) per year.

One of the worst-stricken regions of the Sahel is the Darfur region of the Sudan, where years of drought have exacerbated political and religious unrest. Opposing parties raid Red Cross relief supplies and sabotage the other side's attempts at establishing aid and agriculture, and the people suffer. One of the unpleasant aspects of human nature is that slow-moving, long-lasting disasters like drought tend to bring out the worst in many people. War and corruption often strike drought-plagued regions once relief and foreign aid begins to bring outside food sources into regions. This food may not be enough to feed the whole population, so factions break off and try to take care of their own people. By 1975 about 200,000 people had died, millions of herd animals were dead, and crops and the very structure of society in many Sahel countries was ruined. Children were born brain-damaged because of malnutrition and dehydration, and corruption had set in.

Since the 1980s the region has been plagued with continued more-sporadic drought, but the infrastructure of the region has not returned and the people continue to suffer. Drought led in part to greater civil, ethnic, and religious strife and from 1983–87 the region endured a brutal civil war, when drought drove nomadic Zaghawa and Arab tribes south into ethnic Fur territory. Supply of weaponry and arms to the region increased dramatically, and in 1987 the situation took a political turn for the worse. Twenty-seven nomadic Arab tribes declared an alliance and religious war against the native Zurug (black) and non-Arab tribes of Darfur, who responded by forming their own militias. The Arab tribes were attempting to survive the drought by claiming new land, through killing and driving out whole villages in a campaign of "ethnic cleansing" that has since become one of the world's most horrific examples of genocide. New droughts in 1989, 1990, 1997, 2000, and 2004, continuing to 2008, have caused additional suffering. The Darfur remains parched, and one of the root causes of the civil war and genocide in the region that has by 2008 led to the deaths of hundreds of thousands of people is drought and the slow expansion of the Sahara Desert.

The United States Dust Bowl Period

Drought disasters are not limited to sub-Saharan Africa. Soon after the great U.S. stock market crash of October 1929, the central United States farmland suffered one of its worst drought disasters known, plunging the United States into the Great Depression of the 1930s. Changes in the upper level atmospheric circulation patterns caused upper level dry air to sink into the Great Plains region, and as the air sank it became warmer and drier. The air seemed to soak the moisture right out of the ground, and the crops died, exposing the barren soils to the action of the wind. The winds blew across the Plains states, raising huge clouds of dust known as rollers that moved like thousands-of-feet (hundreds-of-m)-tall steam rollers across the plains. This dust permeated everything, filling homes, lungs, eyes, and every available space with the fine-grained airborne plague. The dust storms became so bad they blocked out the sun, moved across East Coast cities, and even hampered shipping in the Atlantic when they covered ships.

Soon people began leaving the plains in the thousands. Many moved west to California, where the land was available but is now overcrowded and plagued with drought. The Plains States were left in a shambles as the dust bowl days continued into the late 1930s. Numerous studies have indicated that much of the disaster could have been prevented. The weather conditions could not have been changed, and the drought would have occurred, but the severity might have been lessened if the farmers in the region knew that the techniques they were using were actually contributing to the disaster. The farmers were digging deeply into the native soils, disrupting the root systems of existing plants, killing drought-resistant plants, and replacing these with higher-yield crops with shallow root systems. When the drought came, these crops died and the bare soil was exposed and was removed by the strong winds. Even though this area had suffered droughts before, it was mostly not farmed at those times, and the drought-resistant plants native to the region were able to prevent the soil from being eroded by the winds. Now, modern farming techniques are employed in the region, and it should be able to sustain another drought similar to the 1930s without such a huge disaster.

Photo of giant dust storm from dust bowl days in Boise City, Oklahoma, April 15, 1935 *(AP)*

Photo of aftermath dust bowl days in the Midwest, with sand covering farm outhouse in Cimarron, Colorado, April 1936 *(LOC)*

Drought and Water Shortage Brought On by Population Growth

Drought can also be brought on by rapid increases in population, water use (and abuse), and migrations of people into desert or semi-arid regions. Although these regions may never have been able to sustain large populations with their indigenous water supplies, settlement of places like Southern California, the U.S. desert Southwest, and the rapid population expansion in the Middle East all offer examples of how drought-like water shortage conditions are experienced by the people living in these regions.

THE MIDDLE EAST

Drought or basic water shortage coupled with rapid population growth provides for extreme volatility for any region, and the Middle East is one of the most volatile regions in the world. In this region, water shortage issues are coupled with long-standing political and religious differences that have often erupted into conflict and war. The Middle East region, which stretches from North Africa and the Arabian Peninsula through the Levant to Turkey and along the Tigris-Euphrates Valley, has only three major river systems and a few smaller rivers. The population stands at close to 200 million people but is growing rapidly. The Nile has an annual discharge of about 82 billion cubic yards (62.7 billion m³), whereas the combined Tigris-Euphrates system has an annual discharge of 93 billion cubic yards (71 billion m³). Some of the most serious water politics and drought issues in the Middle East arise from the four states that share the relatively small amounts of water of the Jordan River, with an annual discharge of less than 2 billion cubic yards (1.5 billion m³). It has been estimated that with current water usage and population growth, many nations in this region have only a decade left before the agriculture and eventual security of these nations will be seriously threatened.

The region is arid, receiving 1–8 inches (2.5–20 cm) of rain per year, and has many drought years with virtually no rain. The Middle East has a population growth rate of about 3.5 percent per year, one of the fastest in the world, and many countries in the region have inefficient agricultural practices that contribute to the growing problem of desertification in the region. Some of the problems include planting of water-intensive crops, common flooding and furrow methods of irrigation, spraying types of irrigation that waste much of the water to evaporation, and poor management of water and crop resources. These growing demands on the limited water supply, coupled with political strife resulting from shared usage of waterways that flow through multiple countries, has set the region up for a major confrontation over water rights. Many of the region's past and present leaders have warned that water issues may be the cause of the next major conflict in the Middle East. In the words of the late King Hussein of Jordan, water issues "could drive nations of the region to war."

Personal water use by individuals is by necessity much less in countries in the Middle East than in the United States or in other Western countries. For instance, in the United States every American has about 11,000 cubic yards (8,410 m³) of freshwater potential to use each year, whereas citizens of Iraq (pre-war) have about 6,000 cubic yards (4,590 m³), Turkey 4,400 cubic yards (3,364 m³), and Syria about 3,000 cubic yards (2,294 m³). Along the Nile, Egyptians have about 1,200 cubic yards (917 m³) available for each citizen. In the Levant, Israelis have a freshwater potential of 500 cubic yards (382 m³) per person per year, and Jordanians have only 280 cubic yards (214 m³) per year.

People in the Middle East have learned to live without as many showers or freshly watered green lawns as in America and to tolerate a higher level of salt in their drinking water.

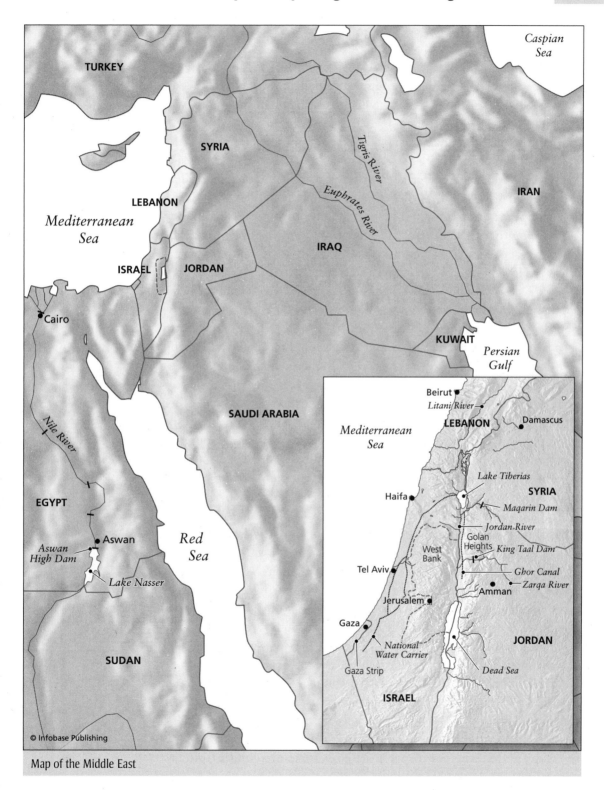

Map of the Middle East

The river Nile, the second longest river on Earth, forms the main water supply for nine north-African nations, and disputes have grown over how to share this water with growing demands. The Blue Nile flows out of the Ethiopian Highlands and meets the White Nile in the Sudan north of Khartoum, then flows through northern Sudan and into Egypt. The Nile is dammed at Aswan, forming Lake Nasser, then flows north through the fertile valley of Egypt to the Mediterranean. Some of the water has been diverted in a project to make a fertile valley east of Lake Nasser, and additional water is diverted in a canal that runs to Sinai. Numerous dams along the Nile, including the large Aswan High Dam, have stopped much of the silt that used to flow down the river, with one result being that the Nile *delta* is not receiving the sediment it needs to remain above sea level, and large areas of the delta are disappearing below sea level.

The Nile is the only major river in Egypt, and nearly all of Egypt's population lives in the Nile Valley. About 3 percent of the nation's arable land stretches along the Nile Valley, but 80 percent of Egypt's water use goes to agriculture in the valley. The government has been attempting to improve agricultural and irrigation techniques, which in many places have not changed considerably for 5,000 years. If the Egyptian agricultural community embraced widespread use of drip irrigation and other modern agricultural practices, then the demands on water could easily be reduced by 50 percent or more. In nearby Israel, drip irrigation projects have changed barren desert landscapes into productive farmland.

The Jordan River basin is host to some of the most severe drought and water shortage issues in the Middle East. Israel, Jordan, Syria, Lebanon, and the Palestinians share the Jordan River water, and the resource is much more limited than water along the Nile or in the Tigris-Euphrates system. The Jordan River is short (100 miles [160 km]), and is made of three main tributaries, each with different characteristics. The Hasbani River has a source in the mountains of Lebanon and flows south to Lake Tiberias, and the Banias flows from Syria into the lake. The smaller Dan River flows from Israel. The Jordan River then flows out of Lake Tiberias, is joined by water from the Yarmuk flowing out of Syria, then flows into the Dead Sea, where any unused water evaporates.

The Jordan River is the source for about 60 percent of the water used in Israel and 75 percent of the water used in Jordan. The other water used by these countries is largely from groundwater aquifers. Israel has almost exclusive use of the coastal aquifer along the Mediterranean shore, whereas disputes arise over use of aquifers from the

West Bank and Golan Heights. These areas are mountainous, get more rain and snowfall than the other parts of the region, and have some of the richest groundwater deposits in the region. Since the 1967 war, Israel has tapped the groundwater beneath the West Bank and now gets approximately 30–50 percent of its water supply from groundwater reserves beneath the mountains of the West Bank. The Palestinians get about 80 percent of their water from this mountain aquifer. A similar situation exists for the Golan Heights, though with lower amounts of reserves. These areas therefore have attained a new significance in terms of regional negotiations for peace and land in the region.

The main problems of water use stem from the shortage of water compared to the population, effectively making drought conditions. The situation is not likely to get better given the alarming 3.5 percent annual population growth rate. Conservation efforts have only marginally improved the water use problem, and it is unlikely that there will be widespread rapid adoption of many of the drip-irrigation techniques used in Israel throughout the region. This is partly because it takes a larger initial investment in drip irrigation than in conventional furrow and flooding types of irrigation systems. Many of the farmers can not afford this investment, even if it would improve their long-term yields and decrease their use of water. Even when existing drip irrigation and greenhouse technology and equipment was left behind by Israeli farmers when they evacuated Gaza, the succeeding days saw widespread looting and destruction of the equipment to sell the parts for fast cash. The result was the loss of a productive agricultural area in the desert and a decimated economy.

Sporadic droughts have made this situation worse in recent years, such that in 1999 Israel cut in half the amount of water it supplies to Jordan, and Jordan declared drought conditions and mandated water rationing. Jordan currently uses 73 percent of its water for irrigation, and if this number could be reduced by adoption of more efficient drip-irrigation, the current situation would be largely in control.

One possible way to alleviate the problem of the drought and water shortage would be to explore for water in unconventional aquifer systems such as fractures or faults, which are plentiful in the region. Many faults are porous and permeable structures that are 30–40 feet (several tens of m) wide and miles (thousands of m) long and deep. They may be thought of as vertical aquifers, holding as much water as conventional aquifers. If these countries were to successfully explore for and exploit water in these structures, the water shortage and regional tensions might be reduced. This technique has proven effective in many other places in the Middle East, Africa, and elsewhere and would probably work here as well. One exploration strategy used by several independent teams is to map the faults and fractures using satellite imagery and do some further analysis in the field and computer modeling to determine which fracture systems might be more likely to yield significant groundwater resources.

A different set of problems plagues the Tigris-Euphrates drainage basin and the countries that share water along their course. There are many political differences between the countries of Turkey, Syria, and Iraq, and the Kurdish people have been fighting for an independent homeland in this region for more than a decade. One of the underlying causes of dispute in this region is also the scarce water supply in a drought-plagued area. Turkey is in the midst of a massive dam construction campaign, with the largest dam being the Attaturk on the Euphrates. Overall, Turkey is spending an estimated 32 billion dollars on 22 dams and 19 hydroelectric plants. The aim is to increase the irrigated land in Turkey by 40 percent and to supply 25 percent of the nation's electricity through the hydroelectric plants. This system of dams also now allows Turkey to control the flow of the Tigris and the Euphrates, and if it pleases, Turkey can virtually shut off the water supply to its downstream neighbors. At present Turkey is supplying Syria and Iraq with what it considers to be a reasonable amount of water, but what Syria and Iraq claim is inadequate. Turkey is currently building a pipeline to bring water to drought-stricken Cyprus. Turkey and Israel are forging new partnerships and have been exploring ways to export water from Turkey and import it to Israel, which could help the drought in the Levant.

UNITED STATES DESERT SOUTHWEST

The history of development the U.S. desert Southwest was also crucially dependent on bringing water resources into this semi-arid region. Much of California was regarded as worthless desert scrub land until huge water projects designed by the Bureau of Land Reclamation diverted rivers and resources from all over the west. Development of the U.S. desert Southwest involves a long history of controversy and corruption associated with the diversion of water resources from Owens Valley, the Trinity River, the Colorado River, and many other western sources and has many parallels to ill-fated societies elsewhere in the history of the world. Now, much of the region has reached a population density that has exceeded the amount of water available to feed the population, and some of the agricultural areas are experiencing increasing saltiness of the soils from evaporation of irrigation waters. The region could become even drier and hotter as the global climate warms, creating a drought crisis that may require people to leave the region.

Map of southwestern United States showing locations of major deserts

Australian lake bed drying up from drought (*Shutterstock*)

Shifting Deserts and Desertification

Deserts expand and contract, reflecting global environmental changes. Many cultures and civilizations on the planet are thought to have met their demise because of desertification of the lands they inhabit and their inability to move with the shifting climate zones. Desertification is defined as the degradation of formerly productive land, and it is a complex process involving many causes. Climates may change, and land use on desert fringes may make fragile ecosystems more susceptible to becoming desert. Among civilizations thought to have been lost to the sands of encroaching deserts are several Indian cultures of the American Southwest such as the Anasazi and many peoples of the Sahel, where up to 250,000 people are thought to have perished in droughts in the late 1960s. Expanding deserts are associated with shifts in other global climate belts, and these shifts too are thought to have brought down several societies. Included are the Mycenaean civilization of Greece and Crete, the Mill Creek Indians of North America, and perhaps even the Viking colony in Greenland. Many deserts are presently expanding, creating enormous drought and famine conditions like those in Ethiopia and Sudan.

Desertification is the invasion of a desert into non-desert areas and is an increasing problem in the southwestern United States, in part due to human activities. This decreases water supply, vegetation, and land productivity; about 10 percent of the land in this country has been converted to desert in the last 100 years, while nearly 40 percent is well on the way. Desertification is also a major global problem, costing hundreds of billions of dollars per year. China estimates that the Gobi Desert alone is expanding at a rate of 950 square miles per year (2,460 km^2), an alarming increase since the 1950s when the desert was expanding at less than 400 square miles (1,036 km^2) per year. The expansion of the Gobi is estimated to cost 6.7 billion dollars a year in China and affects the livelihood of more than 400 million people.

Desertification is a global problem, which could drastically alter the distribution of agriculture and wealth on the globe as the global climate

Sand dunes at Kolmanskop Diamond Ghost Town, Namibia *(Photo Researchers)*

changes. Many deserts are predicted to continue to expand, including the wheat belt of the central United States that will be displaced to Canada. The sub-Saharan Sahel will become part of the Sahara, and the Gobi Desert may expand out of the Alashan and Mongolian Plateaus into northeastern China.

Desertification is a multistage process, beginning with drought, crop and vegetation loss, and then establishment of a desert landscape like those described above. Drought alone does not cause desertification, but misuse of the land during drought greatly increases the chances of a stressed ecosystem reverting to desert. Desertification is associated with a number of other symptoms, including destruction of native and planted vegetation, accelerated and high rates of soil erosion, reduction of surface and groundwater resources, increased saltiness of remaining water supplies, and famine. Desertification can be accelerated by human-induced water use, population growth, and settlement in areas that do not have the water resources to sustain the exogenous population.

Conclusion

Global climate change is causing many deserts of the world to expand, exposing large populations of people to drought and famine conditions. Some of the largest deserts of the world, such as the Sahara, are expanding as the global atmospheric circulation patterns change, and hundreds of thousands of people have perished as crops have failed year after year in the sub-Saharan Sahel. The region has been plunged into civil unrest, partly resulting from drought. Areas in the Middle East have extremely limited water resources, and people in this region use much less water per person than people in European countries and in America. The threat of drought and political/religious difference in the region have created a situation where conflicts could easily break out over drought and water issues as the climate changes. In the U.S. desert Southwest, many new cities and communities have grown in areas with inadequate water supplies, and as the climate warms and the deserts expand, these areas will see increasing pressures on underground water resources and drought conditions. The desert and agricultural belts of America may expand and shift northward as the climate changes.

6

Shrinking Glaciers

At the opposite end of climate extremes from deserts, Earth has experienced at least three major periods of long-term frigid climate and ice ages, interspersed with periods of warm climate. Most glaciers around the world are currently shrinking at rapid rates as a result of global warming. The earliest well-documented ice age is the period of the *"Snowball Earth"* in the late Proterozoic, although there is evidence of several even earlier glaciations. The late Paleozoic saw another ice age lasting about 100 million years, from 350–250 million years ago. The planet entered the present ice age about 55 million years ago. The underlying causes of these different glaciations is varied and includes anomalies in the distribution of continents and oceans and associated currents, variations in the amount of incoming solar radiation, and changes in the atmospheric balance between the amount of incoming and outgoing solar radiation.

Glaciers are any permanent body of ice (recrystallized snow) that shows evidence of gravitational movement. Glaciers are an integral part of the *cryosphere*, which is that portion of the planet where temperatures are so low that water exists primarily in the frozen state. Most glaciers are presently found in the polar regions and at high altitudes. However, at several times in Earth history glaciers have advanced deeply into mid-latitudes and the climate of the entire planet was different. Some models suggest that at one time the entire surface of Earth may have been covered in ice, a state referred to as the Snowball Earth.

Photo of ice wedge clinging to the top of Mount Kilimanjaro, Tanzania *(Corbis)*

Glaciers are dynamic systems, always moving under the influence of gravity and changing drastically in response to changing global climate systems. Thus, changes in glaciers may reflect coming changes in the environment. There are several types of glaciers. Mountain glaciers form in high elevations and are confined by surrounding topography, like valleys. These include cirque glaciers, valley glaciers, and *fiord* glaciers.

Piedmont glaciers are fed by mountain glaciers, but terminate on open slopes beyond the mountains. Some piedmont and valley glaciers flow into open water, bays, or fiords, and are known as tidewater glaciers. Ice caps form dome-shaped bodies of ice and snow over mountains and flow radially outward. Ice sheets are huge, continent-sized masses of ice that presently cover Greenland and Antarctica. These are the largest glaciers on Earth. Ice sheets contain about 95 percent of all the glacier ice on the planet. If global warming continues to melt the ice sheets, sea level could rise by up to 230 feet (66 m). A polar ice sheet covers Antarctica, consisting of two parts that meet along the Transantarctic Mountains. It shows ice shelves, which are thick glacial ice that floats on the sea. These form many icebergs by calving, which move northward into shipping lanes of the Southern Hemisphere.

Polar glaciers form where the mean average temperature lies below freezing, and these glaciers have little or no seasonal melting because they are always below freezing. Other glaciers, called temperate glaciers, have seasonal melting periods, where the temperature throughout the glacier may be at the pressure melting point, when the ice can melt at that pressure and both ice and water coexist. All glaciers form above the snow line, which is the lower limit at which snow remains year-round. It is at sea level in polar regions and at 5,000–6,000 feet (1,525–1,830 m) at the equator (Mount Kilimanjaro in Tanzania has glaciers, although these are melting rapidly).

This chapter examines the formation of glaciers and specific hazards that are caused by glaciation. Glaciers present two main categories of hazards. The first affects those who are working or living on or near glaciers, or transporting goods by sea, river, or land in glacially influenced areas. The second set of hazards is more global in nature and reflects climate change that brings on widespread glaciations. Glaciers also represent sensitive indicators of climate change and global warming, shrinking in times of warming and expanding in times of cooling. Glaciers may be thought of as the "canaries in the coal mine" for climate change. In the Swiss Alps, some ski resorts are covering their slopes with reflective foil in times of non-use in an effort to reduce melting from global warming. The last part of the chapter examines the implications of melting glaciers in terms of climate change.

Formation of Glaciers

Glaciers form mainly by the accumulation and compaction of snow and are deformed by flow under the influence of gravity. When snow falls it is very porous, and with time the pore spaces close by precipitation and compaction. When snow first falls, it has a density of about one-tenth that of ice; after a year or more, the density is transitional between snow and ice, and it is called *firn*. After several years, the ice has a density of 0.9 gm/cm^3, and it flows under the force of gravity. At this point, glaciers are considered to be metamorphic rocks, composed of the mineral ice.

The mass and volume of glaciers are constantly changing in response to the seasons and to global climate changes. The mass balance of a glacier is determined by the relative amounts of accumulation and ablation (mass loss through melting and evaporation or calving). Some years see a mass gain leading to glacial advance, whereas some periods have a mass loss and a glacial retreat. The glacial front or terminus shows these effects.

Glaciers have two main zones, best observed at the end of the summer ablation period. The zone of accumulation is found in the upper parts of the glacier, and is still covered by the remnants of the previous winter's snow. The zone of ablation is below this, and is characterized

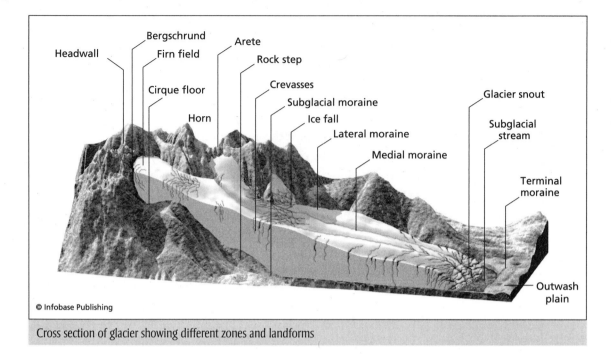

Headwall, Bergschrund, Firn field, Arete, Rock step, Cirque floor, Crevasses, Subglacial moraine, Horn, Ice fall, Lateral moraine, Medial moraine, Glacier snout, Subglacial stream, Terminal moraine, Outwash plain

© Infobase Publishing

Cross section of glacier showing different zones and landforms

by older, dirtier ice, from which the previous winter's snow has melted. An equilibrium line, marked by where the amount of new snow exactly equals the amount that melts that year, separates these two zones.

Movement of Glaciers

When glacial ice gets thick enough, it begins to flow and deform under the influence of gravity. The thickness of the ice must be great enough to overcome the internal forces that resist movement, which depend on the temperature of the glacier. The thickness at which a glacier starts flowing also depends on how steep the slope it is on happens to be—thin glaciers can move on steep slopes, whereas glaciers must become very thick to move across flat surfaces. The flow is by the process of creep, or the deformation of individual mineral grains. This creep leads to the preferential orientation of mineral (ice) grains, forming foliations and lineations, much the same way as in other metamorphic rocks.

Some glaciers develop a layer of meltwater at their base, allowing basal sliding and surging to occur. Where glaciers flow over ridges, cliffs, or steep slopes, their upper surface fails by cracking, forming large, deep crevasses, which can be several hundred feet (100 m) deep. A thin blanket of snow sometimes covers and hides these crevasses, making for very dangerous conditions for people or animals crossing the glacier.

Ice in the central parts of valley glaciers moves faster than ice at the sides, because of frictional drag against the valley walls on the side of the glacier. Similarly, a profile with depth into the glacier would show that they move the slowest along their bases, and faster internally and along their upper surfaces. When a glacier surges, it may temporarily move as fast along its base as it does in the center and top. This is because during surges, the glacier is essentially riding on a cushion of meltwater along the glacial base, and frictional resistance is reduced during surge events. During meltwater enhanced surges, glaciers may advance by as much as several miles in a year. Events like this may happen in response to climate changes. As the climate warms, glacial melting has increased, and many glaciers are surging forward internally even as their snouts are retreating.

Calving refers to a process in which icebergs break off from the fronts of tidewater glaciers or ice shelves. Typically, the glacier will crack with a loud noise that sounds like an explosion, and then a large chunk of ice will splash into the water, detaching from the glacier. Tidewater glaciers retreat rapidly by calving.

Glaciation and Glacial Landforms

Glaciation is the modification of the land's surface by the action of glacial ice. When glaciers move over the land's surface, they plow up the soils, abrade and file down the bedrock, carry and transport the sedimentary load, steepen valleys, then leave thick deposits of glacial debris during retreat.

In glaciated mountains, a distinctive suite of landforms forms from glacial action. *Glacial striations* are scratches on the surface of bedrock, formed when the glacier dragged boulders across the bedrock surface. Roches moutonnées and other asymmetrical landforms form when the glacier plucks pieces of bedrock away from a surface and carries them away. The step faces in the direction of transport. *Cirques* are bowl-shaped hollows that open downstream and are bounded upstream by a steep wall. Frost wedging, glacial plucking, and abrasion all work to excavate cirques from previously rounded mountain tops. Many cirques contain small lakes called tarns, which are blocked by small ridges at the base of the cirque. Cirques continue to grow during glaciation, and where two cirques form on opposite sides of a mountain, a ridge known as an *arête* forms. Where three cirques meet, a steep sided mountain

Rhone glacier, Swiss Alps *(Shutterstock)*

forms, known as a *horn.* The Matterhorn of the Swiss Alps is an example of a glacial carved horn.

Valleys that have been glaciated have a characteristic U-shaped profile, with tributary streams entering above the base of the valley, often as waterfalls. In contrast, streams generate V-shaped valleys. Fiords are deeply indented glaciated valleys that are partly filled by the sea. In many places that were formerly overlain by glaciers, elongate streamlined forms known as *drumlins* occur. These are both depositional features (composed of debris) and erosional (composed of bedrock).

Glacial Transport

Glaciers transport enormous amounts of rock debris, including some large boulders, gravel, sand, and fine silt. The glacier may carry this at its base, on its surface, or internally. Glacial deposits are characteristically poorly sorted or non-sorted, with large boulders next to fine silt. Most of a glacier's load is concentrated along its base and sides, because in these places plucking and abrasion are most effective.

Active ice deposits *till* as a variety of *moraines,* which are ridge-like accumulations of drift deposited on the margin of a glacier. A terminal moraine represents the farthest point of travel of the glacier's terminus.

Glacial debris left on the sides of glaciers forms lateral moraines, whereas where two glaciers meet, their moraines merge and are known as a medial moraine.

Rock flour is a general name for the deposits at the base of glaciers, where they are produced by crushing and grinding by the glacier to make fine silt and sand. *Glacial drift* is a general term for all sediment deposited directly by glaciers, or by glacial meltwater in streams, lakes, and the sea. Till is glacial drift that was deposited directly by the ice. It is a non-sorted random mixture of rock fragments. *Glacial marine drift* is sediment deposited on the seafloor from floating ice shelves or bergs. Glacial marine drift may include many isolated pebbles or boulders that were initially trapped in glaciers on land, then floated in icebergs that calved off from tidewater glaciers. These rocks melted out while over open water and fell into the sediment on the bottom of the sea. These isolated stones are called *dropstones* and are often one of the hallmark signs of ancient glaciations in rock layers that geologists find in the rock record. Stratified drift is deposited by meltwater, and may include a range of sizes, deposited in different fluvial or lacustrine environments.

Glacial erratics are glacially deposited rock fragments that are different from underlying rocks. In many cases the erratics are composed of rock types that do not occur in the area they are resting in, but are found only hundreds or even thousands of miles away. Many glacial

Glacier from Chugach Mountains, Alaska, showing large medial moraine. The toe of the glacier is floating on the water in the fiord, so this is a tidewater glacier. *(T. Kusky)*

erratics in the northern part of the United States can be shown to have come from parts of Canada. Some clever geologists have used glacial erratics to help them find mines or rare minerals that they have found in an isolated erratic—they have used their knowledge of glacial geology to trace the boulders back to their sources following the orientation of glacial striation in underlying rocks. Recently, diamond mines were discovered in northern Canada (Nunavut) by tracing diamonds found in glacial till back to their source region.

Sediment deposited by streams washing out of *glacial moraines* is known as outwash and is typically deposited by braided streams. Many of these form on broad plains known as *outwash plains*. When glaciers retreat, the load is diminished, and a series of outwash terraces may form.

Types of Glacial Hazards

Glaciers present several hazards to those who live near or travel on the ice. Most people do not experience these hazards unless they are on the glacier. Other glacial hazards are more global, including hazards to shipping and rising sea levels caused by melting glaciers.

CREVASSES

Crevasses are extremely hazardous and may be hidden under fresh layers of snow or wind blown drifts. They form most typically over bedrock ridges where the upper surface of the glacier must bend in extension, opening crevasses. Crevasses may be long and narrow but up to several hundred feet (~100 m) deep. There have been a number of accidents on glaciers where hikers, explorers, or natives of glaciated lands have fallen into crevasses. The result is unpleasant and most typically deadly. As a person falls into a crevasse, he or she gets wedged tightly into the bottom of the crevasse, often injured from the fall but still alive. The person's body heat slowly melts an envelope around the person, who sinks slightly deeper into the crevasse. Gradually, the person gets squeezed into a smaller and smaller place and either suffocates from constriction or freezes from hypothermia. Glaciers are typically in remote locations, so death usually results before help can arrive.

CALVING

Tidewater glaciers and ice shelves are prone to spectacular calving events, where huge pieces of the front of the glacier break off and plunge into the water. While calving is one of the more spectacular

Ice block calving off (60 foot [18 m] high) toe of tidewater glacier, Alaska *(T. Kusky)*

events offered by nature, it may also be hazardous. Many a small boat, kayak, and sightseer have been plunged into icy water when they have gotten too close to the front of a tidewater glacier. These glacial fronts are extremely unstable, and may calve at any instant, sending hundreds of thousands of tons of ice plunging into the water in one thunderous crash. This generates large waves, often many tens of feet high, capable of capsizing even moderate-sized boats.

AVALANCHES

Glaciers and recently glaciated valleys have abundant very steep surfaces that are prone to avalanches. Active glaciers are continuously plucking material away from the bases of mountain valleys, causing higher material to avalanche onto the glacier where it gets carried away. Many glaciers are so covered with avalanche debris that they look like dirt-filled valleys. Snow also avalanches onto the main glacial surfaces, adding to the material that may get converted to ice. In areas where glaciers are retreating, recently deglaciated valleys have many avalanches, particularly during wet periods and during shaking by earthquakes.

ICEBERGS AND SEA ICE

Ice that has broken off an ice cap or polar sea or calved off a glacier and is floating in open water is known as *sea ice*. Sea ice presents a serious

SUDDEN DRAINING OF GLACIAL LAKE TERENTIEV, BY GLACIER RETREAT

The Columbia Glacier of south-central Alaska is a tidewater glacier surging at nearly 80 feet (24 m) per day out of the Chugach Mountains into Prince William Sound, releasing two cubic miles (8.3 km³) of ice every year into the Gulf of Alaska. It is one of the world's fastest-shrinking glaciers. The glacier presently covers an area about the size of Los Angeles but has lost nearly six square miles of area (15 km²) since the 1980s. With current rates of ice loss, it will lose another six square miles (15 km²) in 15–20 years and then rise off its base to above sea level.

The retreat of the Columbia Glacier has been associated with an unusual phenomenon, where a deep lake created when the glacier dammed a valley suddenly drained as the valley became open as the glacier retreated. Terentiev Lake, located along the western margin of Columbia Glacier, covers about four square miles (10 km²) and lost about 400 feet (120 m) of water in 1990 as the glacier moved away from the side valley. Geologic evidence suggests that Columbia Glacier has acted as a "cork in a bottle," blocking the valley at several times in the past several thousand years, and has advanced and retreated during this time, alternately draining and filling the lake each time. Observations of the lake have confirmed rapid draining of the lake in successive stages of 115 feet (35 m) sometime between August and October of 1982, 155 feet (47 m) between June and September of 1986, and 226 feet (69 m) between June 1989 and May of 1990. Each of the outbursts for each stage is reported to have occurred in less than one day.

Carbon dating of trees shows that after older similar events, the glacial ice dam lake has refilled, over periods of hundreds of years, between 1650 to 850 years before the present. The cycle repeated again, with observations indicating that the lake drained again on several occasions similar to the successive draining in stages between 1982 and 1990. Along the margins of the lake, streams are cutting through a 40-foot (12-m) thick depositional sequence of glacial gravels and alluvium that includes two buried forest horizons. The alluvium consists of sand, gravel, and clay that decrease in thickness toward the headwaters of the streams. The buried forests contain a basal horizon of black peat, ranging from one to eight inches (3–20 cm) thick, that the tree trunks extend upward from, still in growth positions. The trees are up to 13 feet (4 m) tall, at which point the trunks are truncated by another soil horizon, out of which grows a second, higher layer of paleo-forest. Most trees' trunks are 2–4 inches (4–8 cm) in diameter and still contain bark, suggesting that they were buried by the sand and gravel quickly. The trees in the lower horizon were buried by poorly sorted glacially-derived gravels, sands, and muds, and those in the upper horizon were deposited by more stratified sands and gravels.

The episodic draining of Lake Terentiev by retreat of the ice dam made by Columbia Glacier is preserved in the record of buried forests, gravels, and the present-day bathtub-like rings around the lake. The sequence indicates that the lake has repeatedly filled slowly, then drained catastrophically during a surge of water that gushes out in a crack between the glacier and the bedrock in less than a day. The glacial sediments including the forest and peat layer represent sequential filling of the lake as Columbia Glacier advanced, probably over a period of tens to hundreds of years (based on the tree rings and thickness of the peat horizons). The forests would grow in sediment deposited along the lake shore, then gradually be submerged beneath the cold meltwaters of glacial Lake Terentiev. Burial of the forests by the gravels was sudden as indicated by the trees still in growth position, with bark preserved. The gravels and sands along the margin of the lake are interpreted to have formed during high velocity water flow associated with the sudden draining of the lake. As the water rushed toward the small opening between the glacier and mountain to gush into Prince William Sound, it carried the accumulated sand and gravel from around the lake, depositing ridges of gravel that buried the juvenile forests that had been submerged as the lake was gradually filling.

Photograph of Lake Terentiev, Alaska, showing bathtub like rings indicating the position of the shoreline at different stages of the successive draining of the lake *(T. Kusky)*

hazard to ocean traffic and shipping lanes and has sunk numerous vessels, including the famous sinking of the *Titanic* in 1912, killing 1,503 people.

There are four main categories of sea ice. The first comes from ice that formed on polar seas in the Arctic Ocean and around Antarctica. The ice that forms in these regions is typically about 10–15 feet (3–4 m) thick. Antarctica becomes completely surrounded by this sea ice every winter, and the Arctic Ocean is typically about 70 percent covered in the winter. During summer many passages open up in this sea ice, but during the winter they re-close, forming pressure ridges of ice that may be up to tens of meters high. Recent observations suggest that the sea ice in the Arctic Ocean is thinning dramatically and rapidly, and may soon disappear altogether. The icecap over the Arctic Ocean rotates clockwise, in response to the spinning of Earth. This spinning is analogous to putting an ice cube in a glass, and slowly turning the glass. The ice cube will rotate more slowly than the glass, because it is decoupled from the edge of the glass. About one-third of the ice is removed every year by the East Greenland current. This ice then moves south and becomes a hazard to shipping in the North Atlantic, and it melts and contributes cold fresh water to the thermohaline circulation.

Icebergs from sea ice float on the surface, but between 81 and 89 percent of the ice will be submerged. The exact level that sea ice floats in the water depends on the exact density of the ice, as determined by the total amount of air bubbles trapped in the ice and how much salt got trapped in the ice during freezing.

A second kind of sea ice forms as pack ice in the Gulf of St. Lawrence, along the southeast coast of Canada, in the Bering, Beaufort, and Baltic Seas, in the Seas of Japan and Okhotsk, and around Antarctica. Pack ice builds up especially along the western sides of ocean basins, where cold currents are more common. Occasionally, during cold summers, pack ice may persist throughout the summer.

Several scenarios suggest that new ice ages may begin with pack ice that persists through many summers, gradually growing and extending to lower latitudes. Other models and data show that pack ice varies dramatically with a four- or five-year cycle, perhaps related to sunspot activity and the El Niño–Southern Oscillation (ENSO).

Pack ice presents hazards when it gets so extensive that it effectively blocks shipping lanes, or when leads (channels) into the ice open and close, forming pressure ridges that become too thick to penetrate with ice breakers. Ships attempting to navigate through pack ice have become crushed when leads close, and the ships are trapped. Pack ice has terminated or resulted in disaster for many expeditions to polar seas, most notably Franklin's expedition in the Canadian arctic and Scott's expedition to Antarctica. Pack ice also breaks up, forming many small icebergs, but because these are not as thick as icebergs of other origins they do not present as significant a hazard to shipping.

Pack ice also presents hazards when it drifts into shore, usually during spring break up. With significant winds pack ice can pile up on flat shorelines and accumulate in stacks up to 50 feet (15 m) high. The force of the ice is tremendous and is enough to crush shoreline wharves, docks, buildings, and boats. Pack ice that has blown ashore also commonly pushes up high piles of gravel and boulders that may be 35 feet (11 m) high in places. These ridges are common around many of the Canadian Arctic islands and mainland. Ice that forms initially attached to the shore presents another type of hazard. If it breaks free and moves away from shore, it may carry with it significant quantities of shore sediment, causing rapid erosion of beaches and shore environments.

Pack ice also forms on many high-latitude lakes, and the freeze-thaw cycle causes cracking of the lake ice. When lake water rises to fill the cracks, the ice cover on the lake expands, and pushes over the shoreline, resulting in damage to any structures built along the shore. This is a common problem on many lakes in northern climates and leads to widespread damage to docks and other lakeside structures.

An unusual pack-ice disaster has been occurring in northern Quebec, Canada, along the Ungava Peninsula on the east side of Hudson Bay. A series of dams has been built in Canada along rivers that flow into Hudson Bay, and these dams are used to generate clean hydroelectric energy. The problem that has arisen is that these dammed rivers have annual spring floods, which before the dams were built would flush the pack ice out of Hudson Bay. Since the dams have been built, the annual spring floods are diminished, resulting in the pack ice remaining on Hudson Bay through the short summer. This has drastically changed the summer season on the Ungava Peninsula; as the warm summer winds blow across the ice they pick up cool moist air, and cold fogs now blow across the Ungava all summer. This has drastically changed the local climate and has hindered growth and development of the region.

Icebergs present the greatest danger to shipping. In the Northern Hemisphere most icebergs calve off glaciers in Greenland or Baffin Island, then move south through the Davis Strait into shipping lanes in the North Atlantic off Newfoundland. Some icebergs calve off glaciers adjacent to the Barents Sea, and others come from glaciers in Alaska and British Columbia. In the Southern Hemisphere, most icebergs come from Antarctica, though some come from Patagonia.

Once in the ocean icebergs drift with ocean currents, but because of the Coriolis force are deflected to the right in the Northern Hemisphere, and to the left in the Southern Hemisphere. Most icebergs are about 100 feet to 300 feet (35–92 m) high, and up to about 2,000 feet (610 m) in length. However, in March 2000 a huge iceberg broke off the Ross Ice

Shelf in Antarctica, and this berg was roughly the size of the state of Delaware. It had an area of 4,500 square miles (11,655 km^2), and stuck 205 feet (62 m) out of the water. Icebergs in the Northern Hemisphere pose a greater threat to shipping, as those from Antarctica are too remote and rarely enter shipping lanes. Ship collisions with icebergs have resulted in numerous maritime disasters, especially in the North Atlantic on the rich fishing grounds of the Grand Banks off the coast of Newfoundland.

Icebergs are now tracked by satellite, and ships are updated with their positions so they can avoid any collisions that could prove fatal for the ships. Radio transmitters are placed on larger icebergs to more closely monitor their locations, and many ships now carry more sophisticated radar and navigational equipment that helps track the positions of large icebergs and the ship, so that they avoid collision.

Icebergs also pose a serious threat to oil drilling platforms and sea floor pipelines in high-latitude seas. Some precautions have been taken, such as building seawalls around near-shore platforms, but not enough planning has gone into preventing an iceberg's colliding with and damaging an oil platform, or from one being dragged across the sea floor and rupturing a pipeline.

Glaciers as Sensitive Indicators of Paleoclimate

Glaciers are very sensitive indicators of climate change, as they may melt or advance significantly with relatively small changes in the climate. The planet is presently in an *interglacial period,* where the large ice caps that covered much of North America, Europe, and Asia have only recently (~10,000 years ago) retreated, and there are still many glaciers left on the planet. Some climate change models suggest that the climate can change suddenly in non-linear manners, rapidly plunging Earth into scorchingly hot conditions or into a dark icy winter that may last hundreds of thousands of years. Many glaciers are presently retreating, many rapidly, in response to warming climate conditions. Glaciers also preserve a yearly record of snowfall, preserved as thin layers in the glacial ice. This ice can be sampled with cores and analyzed in laboratories that are able to extract information about the temperatures and other conditions on the planet at the time each snow layer fell. As such, glaciers are important historical records of past climate that can be used to predict future climate trends.

Glaciologists employ a wide variety of techniques to study glaciers, some being concerned with the movement of glaciers, and they may place stakes in various parts of the glacier and around its edges to measure

Glaciers of Greenland that are showing signs of rapid melting. If the Greenland ice cap melts, global sea levels will rise by an additional 23 feet (7 m). (Shutterstock)

their movement with time and to determine how much the glacier has advanced or retreated. Such measurements have improved in accuracy in recent years with the advent of Global Positioning System (GPS) technologies, where sub-centimeter displacements can now be measured.

Remote sensing technologies are also commonly employed for studies of glaciers. Time-series satellite images can show the position of glaciers at various times, so rates of movement can be calculated. Satellite radar and aircraft radar-altimeter data can be used to determine the thickness of snowfall and compare this information with rates of movement to determine the mass balance of glaciers. This information helps determine whether the glacier is experiencing net loss or gain of volume. Other glaciologists are concerned with the physical conditions of deformation of the ice, temperature of the ice with depth, and how the ice may or may not be coupled to the underlying substratum. This information can be important for determining how fast glaciers are able to move and whether rates of movement may stay the same, increase (surge), or decrease with changing conditions.

Many glacial studies are focused on using the isotopic, pollen, and other records in ice cores to determine the paleoclimate history of the past few tens of millions of years of Earth history. To accomplish this goal, glaciologists must drill and extract ice cores and preserve them at subfreezing temperatures for measurement in the laboratory. The ages of the ice cores must be accurately determined, which in some cases can be done by counting down "annual rings" much like counting tree rings. Once the age of the ice layer is determined, glaciologists may analyze the ice, air bubbles trapped in the ice, or other trapped particles that reveal clues to climate history. Numerous ice cores from Greenland and Antarctica are currently being studied to help decipher the climate history of Earth for the past 100,000 years.

Causes of Glaciations

In the last 2.5 billion years, several periods of glaciation have been identified, separated by periods of mild climate similar to that of today. Glaciations seem to form through a combination of several different factors. One of the variables is the amount of incoming solar radiation, and this changes in response to several astronomical and orbital effects, as explained by the Milankovitch cycles that operate on time scales of 100,000 years (eccentricity of Earth's orbit around the Sun), 42,000 years (tilt of Earth's axis from ecliptic), and 11,000 years (wobble, the variation in tilt with time). Another variable is the amount of heat that is retained by the atmosphere and ocean, or the balance between the incoming and outgoing heat. A third variable is the distribution of land masses on the planet. Shifting continents can influence the patterns of ocean circulation and heat distribution, and placing a large continent on one of the poles can cause ice to build up on that continent, increasing the amount of heat reflected back to space and lowering global temperatures in a positive feedback mechanism.

Conclusion

Glaciers are relatively permanent bodies of ice and snow that slowly move under the influence of gravity. Most glaciers of the world are presently shrinking as a result of global warming, and the water released by these melting glaciers is causing global sea level to rise. There are many types of glaciers, including mountain or alpine glaciers, valley glaciers, piedmont glaciers that flow out of mountains onto plains, tidewater glaciers that float on the sea, and large continental ice caps that cover much of Antarctica and Greenland. If all the ice in these glaciers melted, sea levels would rise by 230 feet (66 m). Glaciers pose hazards also to shipping, where icebergs drift into transportation lanes, and to high-latitude shoreline environments where sea-ice can damage shoreline facilities.

7

Past, Present, and Future:
Prediction and Mitigation of Future Climate Change

Previous chapters in this book have described different climate-forcing mechanisms and shown how Earth's climate has been constantly changing since the planet formed. Climate-driving mechanisms include natural variations in Earth's orbit, plate tectonics, supercontinent cycles, massive volcanism, changes in solar luminosity, and changes in the atmosphere that alter its capacity to store and reflect heat. For the past 4.5 billion years, Earth's climate has moved alternately from dominantly temperate climates, to globally hot conditions known as a planetary hothouse, to globally frigid conditions known as a planetary icehouse or Snowball Earth. These changes have all been driven by natural variations in the climate-forcing mechanisms. However, in the past 200 years, humans have been adding significant quantities of greenhouse gases to the atmosphere so that human, or anthropogenic, factors have grown as a new climate-forcing mechanism that rivals or even surpasses many of the natural causes for climate variations. In this chapter, some of the changing conditions on the planet in the past and present are discussed, and predictions for possible future climates of Earth are presented.

Global Hothouses and Global Icehouses: History of Climate Change

At several times in Earth history, large portions of Earth's surface have been covered with huge ice sheets, using much of the water from the planet's oceans. About 10,000 years ago, virtually all of Canada, much

Map of North America showing the extent of the Pleistocene ice sheet and direction of ice flow

of the northern United States, and most of Europe were covered with ice sheets, as was about 30 percent of the world's land mass. These ice sheets lowered sea level by about 320 feet (98 m), exposing the continental shelves, leaving areas where future cities would be, including New York, Washington, and Boston, 100 miles (160 km) from the sea and under or adjacent to significant thicknesses of ice.

Glaciations have happened frequently in the past 55 million years, and could come again at almost any time. In the late 1700s and early

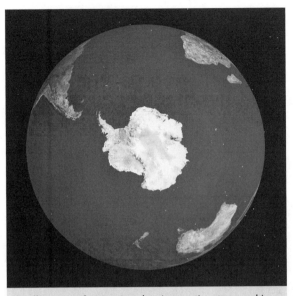

Satellite view of Antarctica, showing continent covered in ice, mimicking conditions of a global icehouse *(SPL)*

1800s, Europe experienced a "little ice age," where many glaciers advanced out of the Alps and destroyed many small villages. Ice ages have occurred at several other times in the ancient geologic past, including in late Paleozoic (about 350–250 million years ago), Silurian (435 million years ago), and late Proterozoic (about 800–600 million years ago). During some glaciations, it is possible that Earth's entire surface temperature was below freezing and covered by ice, forming what is referred to as a Snowball Earth. The causes of these glaciations and conditions that drive the planet in and out of these frozen climate states are the subject of a great amount of research and controversy in climate change studies.

In the late Proterozoic, Earth experienced one of the most profound ice ages in the history of the planet. Isotopic records and geologic evidence suggests that the entire Earth's surface was frozen, though some researchers dispute the evidence and claim that there would be no way for Earth to recover from such a frozen state. In any case it is clear that in the late Proterozoic, during the formation of the supercontinent of Gondwana, Earth experienced one of the most intense Snowball Earth glaciations ever, with the lowest average global temperatures in known Earth history.

One of the longest lasting glacial periods was the late Paleozoic ice age that lasted about 100 million years, indicating a long-term underlying cause of global cooling. Of the variables that operate on these long time scales, it appears that the distribution and orientation of continents seems to have caused the late Paleozoic glaciation. The late Paleozoic saw the amalgamation of the planet's landmasses into the supercontinent of Pangaea. The southern part of Pangaea, known as Gondwana, consisted of present day Africa, South America, Antarctica, India, and Australia. During the drift of the continents in the late Paleozoic, Gondwana slowly moved across the South Pole, and huge ice caps formed on these southern continents during their passage over the pole. The global climate was overall much colder with the subtropical belts becoming very condensed and the polar and subpolar belts expanding to low latitudes.

Photo of Antarctic ice shelf, mimicking appearance of global icehouse *(Shutterstock)*

It seems that during all major glaciations there was a continent situated over one of the poles. Antarctica is now over the South Pole, and this continent has huge ice sheets on it. When continents rest over a polar region they accumulate huge amounts of snow that gets converted into several-mile-thick ice sheets, which reflect more solar radiation back to space, and lower global sea water temperatures and sea levels.

Another factor that helps initiate glaciations is to have continents distributed in a roughly north-south orientation across equatorial regions. Equatorial waters receive more solar heating than polar waters. Continents block and modify the simple east to west circulation of the oceans induced by the spinning of the planet. When continents are present on or near the equator, they divert warm water currents to high latitudes, bringing warm water to higher latitudes. Since warm water evaporates much more effectively than cold water, having warm water move to high latitudes promotes evaporation, cloud formation, and precipitation. In cold high-latitude regions the precipitation falls as snow, which persists and builds up glacial ice.

The late Paleozoic glaciation ended when the supercontinent of Pangaea began breaking apart, suggesting a further link between tectonics and climate. It may be that the smaller land masses could not divert the warm water to the poles anymore, or perhaps enhanced

Dead trees in Dead Vlei, Sossusvlei, Namib Desert, Namibia, showing what global hot house conditions might look like (*Shutterstock*)

volcanism associated with the breakup caused additional greenhouse gases to build up in the atmosphere, raising global temperatures.

The planet began to enter a new glacial period about 55 million years ago, following a 10-million-year-long period of globally elevated temperatures and expansion of the warm subtropical belts into the subarctic. This late Paleocene global hothouse saw the oceans and atmosphere holding more heat than at any other time in Earth history with the exception of the early Precambrian, but temperatures at the equator were not particularly elevated. Instead, the heat was distributed more evenly around the planet such that there were probably fewer violent storms (with a small temperature gradient between low and high latitudes), and overall more moisture in the atmosphere. It is thought that the planet was abnormally warm during this time because of several factors, including the distribution of continents that saw the equatorial region free of continents. This allowed the oceans to heat up more efficiently, raising global temperatures. The oceans warmed so much that the deep ocean circulation changed, and the deep currents that are normally cold became warm. The elevated temperatures melted frozen gases known as methane gas hydrates that accumulate on the sea floor, releasing huge amounts of methane to the atmosphere. Methane is a greenhouse gas, and its increased abundance in the atmosphere trapped solar radiation in the atmosphere, contributing to global warming. In addition, this time saw vast outpourings of mafic lavas in the North Atlantic Ocean realm, and these volcanic eruptions were probably accompanied by the release of large amounts of CO_2, which would have increased the greenhouse gases in the atmosphere, further warming the planet. The global warming during the late Paleocene was so extreme that about 50 percent of all the single-celled organisms living in the deep ocean became extinct.

After the late Paleocene hothouse, Earth entered a long-term cool period that the planet is currently still in, despite the present warming of the past century. This current ice age was marked by the growth of Antarctic glaciers, starting about 36 million years ago until about 14 million years ago, when the Antarctic ice sheet covered most of the continent with several miles (several km) of ice. At this time global temperatures had cooled so much that many of the mountains in the Northern Hemisphere were covered with mountain and piedmont glaciers, similar to those in southern Alaska today. The ice age continued to intensify until at 3 million years ago extensive ice sheets covered the Northern Hemisphere. North America was covered with an ice sheet that extended from northern Canada to the Rocky Mountains, and across the Dakotas, Wisconsin, Pennsylvania, New York, and on the *continental shelf*. At the peak of the glaciation, 18,000–20,000 years ago, about 27 percent of the continent's surfaces were covered with ice. Mid-latitude storm systems were displaced to the south and desert basins of the U.S. southwest. Africa and the Mediterranean received abundant rainfall and hosted many lakes. Sea level was lowered by 425 feet (130 m) to make the ice that covered the continents, so most of the world's continental shelves were exposed and eroded.

The causes of the late Cenozoic glaciation are surprisingly not well known, but seem related to Antarctica's coming to rest over the South Pole and other plate tectonic motions that have continued to separate the once contiguous land masses of Gondwana, changing global circulation patterns in the process. Two of the important events seem to be the closing of the Mediterranean Sea around 23 million years ago and the Panama isthmus at 3 million years ago. These tectonic movements restricted the east-west flow of equatorial waters, causing the warm water to move to higher latitudes, where evaporation promotes snowfall. An additional effect seems to be related to uplift of some high mountain ranges including the Tibetan plateau, which has changed the pattern of the air circulation associated with the Indian monsoon.

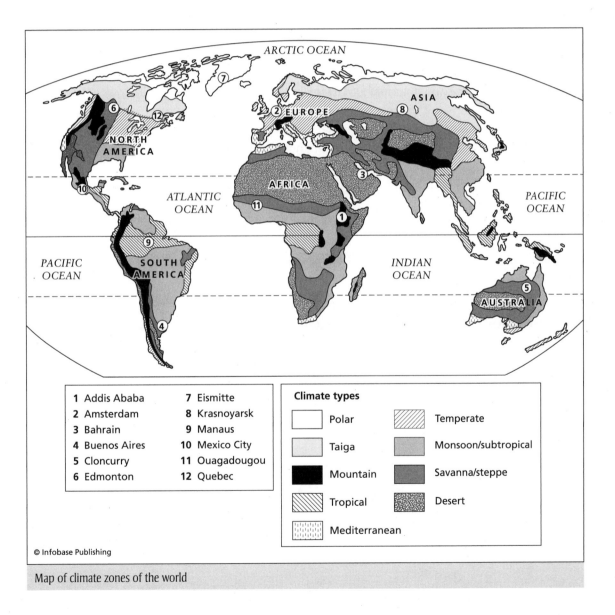

1 Addis Ababa	7 Eismitte
2 Amsterdam	8 Krasnoyarsk
3 Bahrain	9 Manaus
4 Buenos Aires	10 Mexico City
5 Cloncurry	11 Ouagadougou
6 Edmonton	12 Quebec

Climate types

- Polar
- Taiga
- Mountain
- Tropical
- Mediterranean
- Temperate
- Monsoon/subtropical
- Savanna/steppe
- Desert

© Infobase Publishing

Map of climate zones of the world

The closure of the Panama isthmus is closely correlated with the advance of Northern Hemisphere ice sheets, suggesting a causal link. This thin strip of land has drastically altered the global ocean circulation such that there is no longer an effective communication between Pacific and Atlantic Ocean waters, and it diverts warm currents to near-polar latitudes in the North Atlantic, enhancing snowfall and Northern Hemisphere glaciation. Since 3 million years ago, the ice sheets in the Northern Hemisphere have alternately advanced and retreated, apparently in response to variations in Earth's orbit around the Sun and other astronomical effects. These variations change the amount of incoming solar radiation on time scales of thousands to hundreds of thousands of years. Together with the other longer-term effects of shifting continents, changing global circulation patterns, and abundance of greenhouse gases in the atmosphere, most variations in global climate can be approximately explained. This knowledge may help predict where the climate is heading in the future and may help model and mitigate the effects of human-induced or anthropogenic changes to the atmosphere caused by the increased release of greenhouse gases. If the planet is heading into another warm phase and the existing ice on the planet melts, sea level will quickly rise by 210 feet (64 m), inundating many of the world's cities and farmlands. Alternately, if the planet enters a new ice sheet stage, sea levels will be lowered, and the planet's climate zones will be displaced to more equatorial regions.

Predictions of Future Climate Changes by the Intergovernmental Panel on Climate Change

The widespread use of supercomputers and new global data sets has enabled a new generation of projections of what the future climate patterns on the planet will be by the turn of the 21st century in 2100. Most of the models in a range of possible scenarios show projected global average temperature increases of ~0.3°F (0.2°C) per decade as the year 2100 is approached.

Global climate models show that even if the emission of anthropogenic greenhouse gases stopped now, there would still be a warming at about half the predicted rate, due to the delayed and slow response of the ocean system. If nations continue to emit and increase the emission of greenhouse gases (as is likely), then in the 21st century, changes to the global climate system will be larger than those observed in the 20th century.

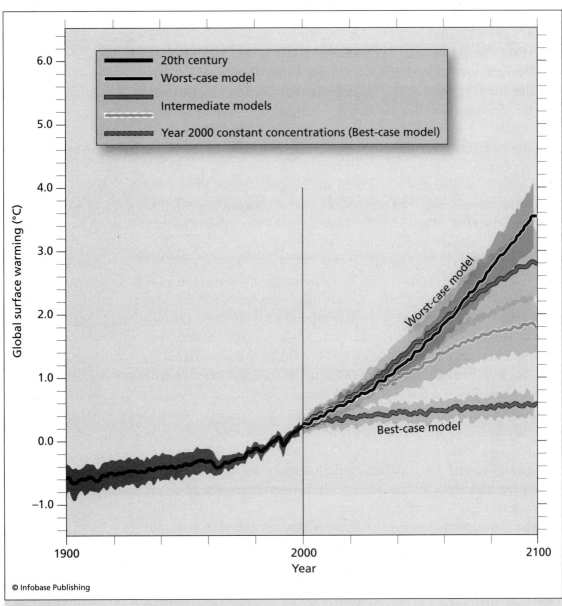

Plot showing future surface warming predicted by Intergovernmental Panel on Climate Change 2007. There is a range of models, based on best- and worst-case scenarios of emissions of greenhouse gases.

A range of different climate change scenarios has been published by many researchers and summarized in the "Climate Change 2007" report issued by the Intergovernmental Panel on Climate Change. The best case scenario with the least change predicts a ~2.5°F (1.8°C) increase in temperature by 2100, whereas the worst case scenario predicts a change of 5–6°F (4°C) by 2100.

As the climate warms, the oceans and land are able to take up less and less carbon dioxide, so more and more remains in the atmosphere at higher temperatures. These complex relationships predict an increasing rate of climate warming and that the climate may continue to warm after 2100. Warming will be greatest over land and in high northern latitudes and least over the Southern Ocean and parts of the North Atlantic Ocean.

Sea levels will continue to rise as the climate warms. By the end of the 21st century, sea level is predicted to rise between seven inches and nearly two feet (0.18–0.59 m). However, if the Greenland and Antarctica ice caps begin to melt any faster, the real sea level rise will be significantly greater.

Snow cover will contract, and much permafrost will melt. Sea ice, particularly in the Arctic Ocean, will shrink dramatically and, in some climate scenarios, disappear by the end of the the 21st century. Extreme weather events, including heat waves and heavy rainfall events, will become more common. Tropical cyclones are likely to become stronger and have greater precipitation, but the number of storms is less certain. Extratropical storm systems will track more poleward as the oceans warm, affecting wider areas.

High latitudes are expected to see increases in the amount of precipitation, while many subtropical belts such as the Sahel will see decreased precipitation, and the Sahara Desert climate belt will expand. Ocean currents, such as the Gulf Stream, may experience sudden and dramatic changes within the 21st century.

Most climate models predict changes through the year 2100, but the changes are predicted to continue for centuries after that, due to the slow response of the ocean system. Further complications in the climate-carbon cycle, such as reduced atmospheric carbon uptake at higher temperatures, will also contribute to the longevity of the global warming caused by anthropogenic greenhouse gases. Even if additional greenhouse gas emission is stopped by 2100, by 2200, sea levels will rise by one to three feet (0.3–0.8 m) and continue for many centuries. It is likely that if greenhouse gases are not curbed, then the Greenland ice sheet will melt catastrophically, contributing another 23 feet (7 m) to sea level rise, to a level not seen since 125,000 years ago. Most global climate models suggest that the Antarctic ice cap will not melt in this time frame.

Whatever level of greenhouse gases is emitted to the atmosphere, these gases will remain in the system for more than a thousand years, contributing to global warming and sea level rise for the entire time period.

Shifting Climate Belts

The dramatic climate changes predicted for the next several centuries mean that the climate belts of the planet will be moving, mostly poleward. The Sahara is presently expanding south into the Sahel, as well as north into the Mediterranean. Likewise, the Gobi Desert is expanding rapidly through Asia and threatens the economy and food supply of a large part of the planet's population in China.

The region of permafrost and ice cover is shrinking poleward rapidly and may disappear altogether from the Northern Hemisphere in a few centuries. More temperate climate belts, such as the wheat belt of the central United States, are also moving north, so that farming areas may move from the United States into central and northern Canada. The desert Southwest of the United States was populated in the last century as a result of finding and transporting water from mountains and rivers in the region to locations of cities and agriculture. Now, it appears that the last century was one of the wettest in the past few hundred years for the region, and the Southwest is entering a new drying spell. There are questions whether or not the water supplies in the region will be able to sustain the current level of population, let alone maintain the growth of the region.

In the geological record there are many examples of areas that were once wet, and then dried up, leaving signs of past wetter climates. Throughout North Africa, Sinai, and Arabia, there are many dry stream beds, dried lakes, and dried rivers buried by sand, that once were filled with flowing water. Analysis of these ancient rivers and dried lakes reveals that many of them date to 320,000 years ago, and formed during wet periods between glacial stages and that the region experienced alternating wet and dry climates throughout the glacial epochs. Other wet periods in the Sahara that lakes and stream sediments formed in have been dated to be 240,000–190,000 years old, 155,000–120,000 years old, and 90,000–65,000 years old. The most recent phase in the eastern Sahara desert lasted from about 10,000 to 5,000 years ago.

Just as climates can change from wet to dry, they can change from dry to wet. In central Alaska north of Mount McKinley, a large field of

Satellite image of coastal desert in Yemen, showing many dry streambeds, or wadis, many of which initially formed when the climate was wetter several thousand years ago (Photo Researchers)

giant sand dunes is being slowly overgrown by evergreen trees. These sand dunes and associated loess deposits are late Quaternary in age and are thought to have formed during glacial stages when the area was dry and regional winds brought the sand from the west and from the south. Now, during the interglacial stage, sea levels are higher and the region is humid.

Mitigation of Climate Change
If immediate and dramatic steps are taken by the nations of the world to reduce the emission of anthropogenic greenhouse gases, then some

Photo of Great Kobuk sand dunes in Kobuk Valley National Park, central Alaska *(Alamy)*

of the predicted future climate change may be reduced from some of the "worst case" to some of the "better case" scenarios outlined by the Intergovernmental Panel on Climate Change. It is inevitable that climate change and its consequences are happening and will continue, but the severity of the effects may be reduced over time by adopting different but economically feasible industrial, agricultural, and personal practices than are currently in widespread use.

Meeting emission goals for greenhouse gases is a complex process, involving the developed and developing nations of the world. Adopting climate change policies in industry may drive new technologies that are greener and produce less atmospheric CO_2 and other gases. Previous attempts at lowering greenhouse emissions, such as the Kyoto Protocol, allowed trading of carbon credits between nations to allow large carbon producers economic trades with other nations and time to adjust to the protocols. However, not all countries signed the Kyoto standards.

CARBON SEQUESTRATION

Carbon dioxide is one of the major greenhouse gases whose rise in concentration in the atmosphere is responsible for the global rise in temperature during the past 200 years. Carbon dioxide is produced by many processes, both natural and by humans. It is the rapid rise in human, or anthropogenic, CO_2 that is thought to be mainly responsible for the current episode of global warming. To reduce global warming, it will be necessary to reduce the release of CO_2 to the atmosphere, so that the system can gradually recover and slow global warming. There are several ways that the release of carbon dioxide to the atmosphere can be reduced. Most CO_2 is produced through the combustion of fossil fuels. One way to reduce CO_2 release to the atmosphere therefore is to use energy more efficiently and wisely and to increase use of low-carbon and carbon-free fuels and technologies. These include renewable green energy sources such as nuclear power, solar and wind energy, geothermal power, and tidal and current power. A new technology for managing carbon is being developed by the U.S. Department of Energy and many other countries and industries around the world. This new promising technology is called *carbon sequestration*.

Carbon sequestration is basically a group of processes that enable long-term storage of carbon in the terrestrial biosphere, in the oceans, or deep underground, effectively isolating that carbon from the atmosphere. Carbon sequestration can be done in a number of different ways. Some of these processes enhance natural processes, whereas others are basically advanced ways of disposing of the carbon.

Carbon sequestration may be done in underground reservoirs. The basic idea is that carbon dioxide can be captured from power plants and other carbon-producing industries, and then injected underground into porous geological formations. Although this technology has existed for some time, it is nowhere in widespread use, and exists as a potential way to greatly reduce greenhouse gas emissions to the atmosphere. Simple carbon sequestration technologies that already exist could reduce the emissions from each plant that uses this technique by 80–90 percent. However, the energy required to

Many sectors of industry and agriculture need to respond to reducing the emissions of several greenhouse gases. One of the promising developing technologies is that of carbon sinks, either burying the carbon in the ground or in other carbon sinks isolated from the atmosphere system. This new technology of carbon sequestration is described in the sidebar above.

Education and changes in lifestyle choices have the potential to dramatically change greenhouse gas emissions. Consumer choice in using environmentally friendly or green technologies can drive industry to move toward products that produce fewer greenhouse gases, lowering emissions. Urban and community planning, where new communities include lower transportation distances, improved energy efficiency, and alternative energy, farming, and waste technologies have potential to continue to reduce emissions. As sea level rises and large sectors of the population are forced to move, community planning will become an

implement this carbon sequestration would increase the fuel needs of each plant by 11–40 percent, increasing the cost of energy from each plant that uses this technology by 20–90 percent.

Some novel ways of sequestering carbon involve enhancing the natural carbon sequestration of the terrestrial biosphere cycle through removal of CO_2 from the atmosphere by plants and storing the carbon in biomass and soils. Research is being funded through the Department of Energy to understand better the biological and ecological processes of the formation of organic matter in soils in different terrestrial ecosystems, particularly wetlands, and searching for ways to enhance these processes. Different topics that are investigated include increasing the capture of CO_2 from the atmosphere by plants, retaining carbon and transforming it to soil organic matter, reducing the emission of CO_2 from soils, and investigating the possibility of increasing the use of deserts and degraded lands to sequester carbon.

One of the largest potential reservoirs for sequestering carbon is the oceans. Techniques are being developed that can increase the uptake of CO_2 by the oceans through the fertilization of phytoplankton with nutrients and by directly injecting pure CO_2 streams into the oceans to depths below .62 miles (1 km). The CO_2 being targeted for direct injection would come from power plants and other industrial CO_2 producers, reducing the emission to the atmosphere. Research by the Department of Energy is still focusing on determining if there may be any unseen environmental consequences of sequestering carbon deep in the oceans and how effective this process may be.

A final way that carbon may be sequestered and isolated from the atmosphere is by sequencing and designing microbes that aid in carbon sequestration, searching for the genetic components that organisms use to capture greenhouse gases. There are organisms known as extremophiles that presently live in hot environments and ingest methane, sequestering carbon, and giving off hydrogen gas as a byproduct. Since much of the living material on the planet that sequesters carbon is microbial, research into enhancing microbial carbon sequestration is a promising field for potentially reducing anthropogenic CO_2 in the atmosphere and its heating effects.

increasingly important element in decades to come. Eventually these techniques will lead to increased agricultural production and decreased stress on ecosystems.

Development and investment in new energy technologies and infrastructure will promote lower production of greenhouse gases and serve to increase the energy security of nations. Investments in new energy technologies are expected to surpass 30 trillion U.S. dollars by 2030, including the use of renewable energy sources such as solar, wind, nuclear, waves, *tides,* currents, and hydrothermal sources. As easily accessible oil resources become increasingly scarce, it is important that industry adopts carbon capture and storage technologies as the fossil-fuel industry moves into resources with higher carbon contents, otherwise greenhouse gas emission will increase. Underground carbon capture and storage is a rapidly developing technology that has potential to lower emission of greenhouse CO_2, especially from fossil fuel mining. Technologies should be developed that are able to extinguish underground coal fires, as CO_2 released from coal fires in China alone rival the amount of CO_2 emitted by all the automobiles in the United States.

Improved fuel efficiency of cars and trucks is essential and within reach with existing and developing technologies. *Biofuels* may play an important role in this regard, but biofuels may have environmental impacts of their own that need to be addressed. Lifestyle and industrial shifts to wider use of railroads and multi-passenger vehicles would lower CO_2 emissions, as would urban planning that would help decrease distances traveled and offer opportunities for wider use of light rail and non-motorized transportation modes. Aviation emissions are significant and can be reduced by better air traffic management.

Wider adoption of green building technologies can reduce the emission of greenhouse gases from this sector of the economy by at least 30 percent by 2030, and more by the end of the century. However, many developing countries will not be able to afford the initial investment in green building construction, despite the longer-term economic benefit.

New industrial facilities in developing countries are tending to move toward adopting new technologies with lower emissions, but many old highly inefficient industrial facilities exist in both developed and developing countries. These facilities are in drastic need of upgrade and offer considerable opportunities for reduction in greenhouse gas emission.

The agricultural sector can move toward more sustainable agricultural practices, with synergy between the agriculture and developing soils for carbon sequestration. Some widespread agricultural practices currently expose the carbon soil to atmospheric loss. Reduction of other agricultural greenhouse gases such as methane and nitrous oxide can be achieved through land use changes and other implementations. Using feedstocks for biofuels has benefits and drawbacks and must be managed with land and water use and maintenance of sufficient feedstock for fiber production.

Forest management strategies such as reduction in deforestation in tropical regions can significantly help by increasing the carbon sink, reducing the emissions from deforestation, with co-benefits such as employment for local people in the eco-tourism business, preservation of ecosystems and biodiversity, and a renewable energy supply. Other sectors of the economy can also be managed better to improve the environment, including management of the waste sector to minimize wastes and wastewater and research into geo-engineering options for developing technologies that potentially remove CO_2 from the atmosphere, sequestering it in the oceans or on land.

Longer-term climate mitigation, beyond the year 2100, will require that emission of greenhouse gases not only stop at current levels but be reduced further to lower levels. This will require long-term development of energy-efficient technologies, changes in lifestyles and land use patterns, and investment at national scales in green industrial technologies. National and international policies still need to be developed to balance environmental concerns over greenhouse gas emissions with cost, equity and distribution, and the feasibility of proposed steps to reduce greenhouse gas emissions. The world will continue to develop but must develop new pathways of development to ensure that global growth is sustainable.

Conclusion

Earth's climate has oscillated between hot and cold states for billions of years, due to a variety of climate-forcing mechanisms. Some climates, known as global icehouses or Snowball Earth, have been much colder than the present, and other climate intervals, known as hothouses, have been much warmer than the present. Until recently these climate variations have all been driven by natural variations in Earth's orbit, the solar luminosity, the concentration of gases in the atmosphere, and plate tectonics and volcanism. In the past 200 years humans have injected so much carbon dioxide and other greenhouse gases into the atmosphere that the climate is warming rapidly as a result.

Global climate models predict that the climate will continue to warm for at least several hundred and probably at least several thousand years. The planet may have an average temperature that is three to five degrees hotter by the year 2100, changing many climate patterns across the globe. Deserts will expand, Arctic ice and permafrost will largely melt, and sea levels will rise by seven inches to nearly two feet (0.18–0.59 m), or as many as 23 more feet (7 m) if the Greenland ice cap melts catastrophically.

Global warming cannot be stopped. Even a major event such as a catastrophic volcanic eruption that places large amounts of aerosols into the atmosphere would likely lower temperatures only for a year or two. Nonetheless, the warming can be slowed by reducing the emission of greenhouse gases to the atmosphere and beginning programs of carbon sequestration to isolate carbon from the atmosphere system. Green energy technologies such as solar, wind, nuclear, tidal, and geothermal sources should be employed, and people's lifestyles need to change to use less fossil fuels. As sea levels rise and hundreds of millions of people are displaced from the current coastlines, new cities and communities should be planned to be more energy efficient, involving less traveling, using green energy technology in building, utilizing sustainable agriculture, and recycling wastes and water.

8

Summary

Earth's climate changes on many different time scales, ranging from tens of millions of years to decadal and even shorter time scale variations. In the last 2.5 billion years, several periods of glaciation have been identified, separated by periods of mild climate similar to that of today. Other periods are marked by global hothouse type conditions, when Earth had a very hot and wet climate, approaching that of Venus. These dramatic climate changes are caused by a number of different factors that exert their influence on different time scales. One of the variables is the amount of incoming solar radiation, which changes in response to several astronomical effects such as orbital tilt, eccentricity, and wobble. Changes in the incoming solar radiation in response to changes in orbital variations produce cyclical variations known as Milankovitch cycles. Another variable is the amount of heat that is retained by the atmosphere and ocean, or the balance between the incoming and outgoing heat. A third variable is the distribution of landmasses on the planet. Shifting continents can influence the patterns of ocean circulation and heat distribution, and placing a large continent on one of the poles can cause ice to build up on that continent, increasing the amount of heat reflected back to space and lowering global temperatures in a positive feedback mechanism. Continental collisions and the formation of supercontinents can expose many rocks to weathering, which draws CO_2 out of the atmosphere and lowers global temperatures. Supercontinent breakup can be associated with large amounts of undersea volcanism, that emits huge amounts of CO_2 into the atmosphere, causing global warming.

Shorter-term climate variations include those that operate on periods of thousands of years, and shorter, less regular decadal scale variations. Both of these relatively short-period variations are of most concern to humans, and considerable effort is being extended to understand their causes and to estimate the consequences of the current climate changes the planet is experiencing. Great research efforts such as that of the Intergovernmental Panel on Climate Change are being expended to understand the climate history of the last million years and to help predict the future.

Variations in formation and circulation of ocean waters may cause some of the thousands of years to decadal scale variations in climate. Thermohaline circulation is influenced by the distribution of continents and by the balance between freshwater released from melting glaciers and evaporation in different parts of the globe. If one factor changes, such as widespread melting of Arctic ice, then the patterns of thermohaline circulation can change, perhaps in a matter of years.

Changes in the thermohaline circulation rigor have also been related to other global climate changes. Droughts in the Sahel and elsewhere are correlated with periods of ineffective or reduced thermohaline circulation, because this reduces the amount of water drawn into the North Atlantic, in turn cooling surface waters and reducing the amount of evaporation. Reduced thermohaline circulation also reduces the amount of water that upwells in the equatorial regions, in turn decreasing the amount of moisture transferred to the atmosphere, reducing precipitation at high latitudes.

Atmospheric levels of greenhouse gases such as CO_2 and atmospheric temperatures show a correlation to variations in the thermohaline circulation patterns and production of cold bottom waters. CO_2 is dissolved in warm surface water and transported to cold surface water, which acts as a sink for the CO_2. During times of decreased flow from cold, high-latitude surface water to the deep ocean reservoir, CO_2 can build up in the cold polar waters, removing it from the atmosphere and decreasing global temperatures. In contrast, when the thermohaline circulation is vigorous, cold oxygen-rich surface waters downwell and dissolve buried CO_2 and even carbonates, releasing this CO_2 to the atmosphere and increasing global temperatures.

Major volcanic eruptions inject huge amounts of dust into the troposphere and stratosphere, where it may remain for several years, reducing incoming solar radiation and resulting in short-term global cooling. For instance, the eruption of Tambora volcano in Indonesia in 1815 resulted in global cooling and the year without a summer in Europe. The location of the eruption is important, as equatorial eruptions may result in global cooling, whereas high-latitude eruptions may cool only one hemisphere.

It is clear that human activities are changing the global climate, primarily through the introduction of greenhouse gases such as CO_2 into the atmosphere while cutting down tropical rain forests that act as sinks for the CO_2 and put oxygen back into the atmosphere. The time scale of observation of these human, also called anthropogenic, changes is short but the effect is clear, with a nearly one degree change in global temperature measured for the past few decades. The increase in temperature will lead to more water vapor in the atmosphere, and since water vapor is also a greenhouse gas, this will lead to a further increase in temperature. Many computer-based climate models are attempting to predict how much global temperatures will rise as a consequence of our anthropogenic influences and what effects this temperature rise will have on melting of the ice sheets (which could be catastrophic), sea level rise (perhaps 30–60 feet [tens of meters] or more), and runaway greenhouse temperature rise (which is possible).

Climate changes are difficult to measure, partly because the instrumental and observational records go back only a couple of hundred years in Europe. From these records, global temperatures have risen by about one degree since 1890, most notably between 1890 and 1940, and again since 1970. This variation however, is small compared to some of the other variations induced by natural causes, and some scientists argue that it is difficult to separate anthropogenic effects from the background natural variations. Rainfall patterns have also changed in the past 50 years, with declining rainfall totals over low latitudes in the Northern Hemisphere, especially in the Sahel, which has experienced major droughts and famine. However, high-latitude precipitation has increased in the same time period. These patterns all relate to a general warming and shifting of the global climate zones to the north. The world's alpine glaciers are shrinking and disappearing, while the desert belts are expanding. Nations of the world need to begin to plan for large-scale environmental changes that will affect patterns of agriculture, mass movements of millions of people, flooding of coastal zones, and shifting deserts, glaciers, and climate belts.

Appendix

The Geologic Timescale

Era	Period	Epoch	Age (millions of years)	First Life-forms	Geology
		Holocene	0.01		
	Quaternary				
		Pleistocene	3	Humans	Ice age
Cenozoic		Pliocene	11	Mastodons	Cascades
		Neogene			
		Miocene	26	Saber-toothed tigers	Alps
	Tertiary	Oligocene	37		
		Paleogene			
		Eocene	54	Whales	
		Paleocene	65	Horses, Alligators	Rockies
	Cretaceous		135		
				Birds	Sierra Nevada
Mesozoic	Jurassic		210	Mammals	Atlantic
				Dinosaurs	
	Triassic		250		
	Permian		280	Reptiles	Appalachians
	Pennsylvanian		310		Ice age
				Trees	
	Carboniferous				
Paleozoic	Mississippian		345	Amphibians	Pangaea
				Insects	
	Devonian		400	Sharks	
	Silurian		435	Land plants	Laurasia
	Ordovician		500	Fish	
	Cambrian		544	Sea plants	Gondwana
				Shelled animals	
			700	Invertebrates	Rodinia
Proterozoic			2500	Metazoans	
			3500	Earliest life	
Archean			4000		Oldest rocks
			4600		Meteorites

Glossary

abrasion—A process that occurs when particles of sand and other sizes are blown by the wind and impact each other.

acid rain—Rain or other form of precipitation that has acidic components leading to a pH of less than seven. The extra acidity in acid rain comes from the reaction of air pollutants, mostly sulfur and nitrogen oxides, with water to form strong acids like sulfuric and nitric acid.

aerosol—Microscopic droplets or airborne particles that remain in the atmosphere for at least several hours.

alluvial fans—Coarse-grained deposits of alluvium that accumulate at the fronts of mountain canyons.

anthropogenic—Human-induced factors in the environment.

aquifers—Any body of permeable rock or regolith saturated with water through which groundwater moves.

Archaean—The oldest eon of geological time, ranging from 4.5 billion years ago until 2.5 billion years ago.

arête—Knife-edged ridge that forms where two cirques intersect.

atmosphere—The disk of air that surrounds Earth, held in place by gravity. The most abundant gas is nitrogen (78 percent), followed by oxygen (21 percent), argon (0.9 percent), carbon dioxide (0.036 percent), and minor amounts of helium, krypton, neon, and xenon.

atmospheric pressure—The force per unit area (similar to weight) that the air above a certain point exerts on any object below it.

aurora—Glows of light sometimes visible in high latitudes around both the North and South Poles. They are formed by interaction of the solar wind with Earth's magnetic field.

beach—Accumulations of sediment exposed to wave action along a coastline.

biofuels—Fuels such as methane that are produced from renewable biological resources, including recently living organisms, such as plants, and their metabolic byproducts, such as manure.

biosphere—Collection of all organisms on Earth.

calving—The process where large blocks of ice plunge off the front of a tidewater glacier and fall into the sea making icebergs.

carbonate—A sediment or sedimentary rock containing the carbonate (CO_3^{-2}) ion. Typical carbonates include limestone and dolostone.

carbon sequestration—A group of processes that enable long-term storage of carbon in the terrestrial biosphere, in the oceans, or deep underground, effectively isolating that carbon from the atmosphere.

chemical weathering—Decomposition of rocks through the alteration of individual mineral grains.

chlorofluorocarbons—A group of inert, nontoxic, and easily liquefied chemicals that were widely used in refrigeration. When released to the atmosphere they become long-lived greenhouse gases that contain carbon, hydrogen, fluorine, and chlorine, increasing in atmospheric concentration as a result of human activity. Chlorofluorocarbons are thought to cause depletion of the atmospheric ozone layer.

cirques—Bowl-shaped hollows that open downstream and are bounded upstream by a steep wall.

climate—The average weather of an area.

climate change—The phenomena where global temperatures, patterns of precipitation, wind, and ocean currents change in response to human and natural causes.

continental shelf—Generally fairly flat areas on the edges of the continents, underlain by continental crust and having shallow water. Sedimentary deposits on continental shelves include muds, sands, and carbonates.

convergent boundaries—Places where two plates move toward each other, resulting in one plate sliding beneath the other when a dense oceanic plate is involved, or collision and deformation, when continental plates are involved. These types of plate boundaries may have the largest of all earthquakes.

Coriolis effect—A force that causes any freely moving body in the Northern Hemisphere to veer to the right and in the Southern Hemisphere to the left.

cryosphere—That portion of the planet where temperatures are so low that water exists primarily in the frozen state.

cyclone—A tropical storm, equivalent to a hurricane, that forms in the Indian Ocean.

deflation—A process whereby wind picks up and removes material from an area, resulting in a reduction in the land surface.

delta—Low flat deposits of alluvium at the mouths of streams and rivers that form broad triangular or irregular shaped areas that extend into bays, oceans, or lakes. They are typically crossed by many distributaries from the main river and may extend for a considerable distance underwater.

desert—An area characterized by receiving less than one inch (2.5 cm) of rain each year over an extended period of time.

desertification—Conversion of previously productive lands to desert.

desert pavement—A long-term stable surface in deserts characterized by pebbles concentrated along the surface layer.

diurnal cycle—Variations in the daily temperature.

divergent boundaries—Margins where two plates move apart, creating a void that is typically filled by new oceanic crust that wells up to fill the progressively opening hole.

dropstones—Isolated pebbles or boulders in marine sediments, deposited when rocks trapped in floating icebergs melted out of the ice and dropped to the seafloor.

drought—A prolonged lack of rainfall in a region that typically gets more rainfall.

drumlins—Teardrop-shaped accumulations of till that are up to about 150 feet (50 m) in height and tend to occur in groups of many drumlins. These have a steep side that faces in the direction that the glacier advanced from and a back side with a more gentle slope. Drumlins are thought to form beneath ice sheets and record the direction of movement of the glacier.

dune—Low wind-blown mounds of sand or granular material, with variable size and shape depending on sand supply, vegetation, and wind strength.

eccentricity—An astronomical measure of how elliptical the orbit of Earth (or other planet) is around the Sun.

ecosystem—A collection of the organisms and surrounding physical elements that together are unique to a specific environment.

El Niño—One of the better-known variations in global atmospheric circulation patterns that causes a warm current to move from the western Pacific to the eastern Pacific and has global consequences in terms of changes in weather patterns. Full name is El Niño–Southern Oscillation (ENSO).

epeirogenic—A term referring to the vertical movements of continents.

eustatic sea level changes—Sea levels may rise or fall for local reasons, such as tectonic subsidence, or global reasons, such as melting of glaciers. When the sea level change can be shown to be global in scale it is called eustatic.

fiords—Glacially carved steep-sided valleys that are open to the sea.

firn—Frozen water that is in transition in density between snow and ice.

flash flood—Floods that rise suddenly, typically as a wall of water in a narrow canyon.

flood basalt—Anomalously thick accumulations of dark lava, variously known as flood basalts, traps, or large igneous provinces.

glacial drift—A general term for all sediment deposited directly by glaciers or by glacial meltwater in streams, lakes, and the sea.

glacial erratic—Glacially deposited rock fragments with compositions different from underlying rocks.

glacial marine drift—Sediment deposited on the seafloor from floating ice shelves or bergs. It may include many isolated pebbles or boulders that were initially trapped in glaciers on land, then floated in icebergs that calved off from tidewater glaciers.

glacial moraine—Piles of sand, gravel, and boulders deposited by a glacier.

glacial period—A time in Earth history characterized by great ice sheets that moved across the continents.

glacial rebound—When an ice sheet melts, the weight of the ice is removed from the continent, which then rises upward (rebounds) in response to the reduced weight.

glacial striations—Scratches on the surface of bedrock, formed when the glacier dragged boulders across the bedrock surface.

glacier—Any permanent body of ice (recrystallized snow) that shows evidence of gravitational movement.

global warming—A gradual warming of the planet surface (land, air, and sea) typically in response to increases in greenhouse gases in the atmosphere.

Gondwana—A late Proterozoic to late Paleozoic supercontinent of the Southern Hemisphere that included present day Africa, South

America, Australia, India, Arabia, Antarctica, and many small fragments.

Great Ice Ages—A term to refer to the late Pleistocene glaciation.

greenhouse effect—A phenomenon where Earth's climate is sensitive to the concentrations of certain gases in the atmosphere and heats up when the concentration of these gases is increased.

greenhouse gases—Gases such as CO_2 that when built up in the atmosphere tend to keep solar heat in the atmosphere, resulting in global warming.

groundwater—All the water contained within spaces in bedrock, soil, and regolith.

Hadley Cell—Belts of air that encircle Earth, rising along the equator, dropping moisture as they rise in the tropics. As the air moves away from the equator at high elevations, it cools, becomes drier, and then descends at 15–30°N and S latitude where it either returns to the equator or moves toward the poles.

Heinrich Events—Specific intervals in the sedimentary record showing ice-rafted debris in the North Atlantic.

horn—Peak that forms where three cirques meet.

hothouse—A time when the global climate was characterized by very hot conditions for an extended period.

hot spot—An area of unusually active magmatic activity that is not associated with a plate boundary. Hot spots are thought to form above a plume of magma rising from deep in the mantle.

hurricane—A tropical cyclone in which an organized group of thunderstorms rotates about a central low pressure center and has a sustained wind speed of 74 miles per hour (118 kph) or greater.

hydrosphere—A dynamic mass of liquid, continuously on the move between the different reservoirs on land and in the oceans and atmosphere. The hydrosphere includes all the water in oceans, lakes, streams, glaciers, atmosphere, and groundwater, although most water is in the oceans.

inselbergs—Steep-sided mountains or ridges that rise abruptly out of adjacent monotonously flat plains in deserts.

interglacial period—The present climate epoch is one characterized as being between advances and retreats of major continental ice sheets. The glaciers could return, or global warming could melt the remaining polar ice taking the planet out of the glacial epoch.

Intergovernmental Panel on Climate Change—The IPCC is a scientific intergovernmental body set up by the World Meteorological

Organization (WMO) and by the United Nations Environment Program (UNEP). The IPCC is open to all member countries of WMO and UNEP. Governments participate in plenary sessions of the IPCC where main decisions about the IPCC work program are taken and reports are accepted, adopted, and approved. They also participate in the review of IPCC Reports. The IPCC includes hundreds of scientists from all over the world who contribute to the work of the IPCC as authors, contributors, and reviewers. As a United Nations body, the IPCC work aims at the promotion of the United Nations human development goals.

jet stream—High-level, narrow, fast moving currents of air that are typically thousands of miles (km) long, hundreds of miles (km) wide, and several miles (km) deep.

landslide—A general name for any downslope movement of a mass of bedrock, regolith, or a mixture of rock and soil, commonly used to indicate any mass wasting process.

lava—Magma, or molten rock that flows at the surface of Earth.

leeward—The side of a mountain facing away from oncoming winds.

limestone—A sedimentary carbonate rock made predominantly of the mineral calcite ($CaCO_3$).

lithosphere—Rigid outer shell of Earth that is about 75 miles (125 km) thick under continents and 45 miles (75 km) thick under oceans. The basic theorem of plate tectonics is that the lithosphere of Earth is broken into about twelve large rigid blocks or plates that are all moving relative to one another.

loess—Silt and clay deposited by wind.

magma—Molten rock at high temperature. When magma flows on the surface it is known as lava.

mass extinction—Times when large numbers of species and individuals within species die off. Mass extinction events are thought to represent major environmental catastrophes on a global scale. In some cases these mass extinction events can be tied to specific likely causes, such as meteorite impact or massive volcanism, but in others their cause is unknown. Earth's biosphere has experienced five major and numerous less-significant mass extinctions in the past 500 million years (in the Phanerozoic era). These events occurred at the end of the Ordovician, in the late Devonian, at the Permian/Triassic boundary, the Triassic/Jurassic boundary, and at the Cretaceous/Tertiary (K/T) boundary.

mesosphere—Region of the atmosphere that lies above the stratosphere, extending between 31 and 53 miles.

mid-ocean ridge system—A 40,000-mile- (65,000-km-) long mountain ridge that runs through all the major oceans on the planet. The mid-ocean ridge system includes vast outpourings of young lava on the ocean floor and represents places where new oceanic crust is being generated by plate tectonics.

Milankovitch cycles—Variations in Earth's climate that are caused by variations in the amount of incoming solar energy, induced by changes in Earth's orbital parameters including tilt, eccentricity, and wobble.

monsoon—A wind system that influences large regions and has seasonally persistent patterns with pronounced changes from wet to dry seasons.

moraine—Ridge-like accumulations of glacial drift deposited at the edges of a glacier. Terminal moraines mark the farthest point of travel of a glacier, whereas lateral moraines form along the edges of a glacier.

mudflow—A downslope flow that resembles a debris flow, except it has a higher concentration of water (up to 30 percent), which makes it more fluid, with a consistency ranging from soup to wet concrete. Mudflows often start as a muddy stream in a dry mountain canyon, which as it moves it picks up more and more mud and sand, until eventually the front of the stream is a wall of moving mud and rock.

outwash plain—A broad plain in front of a melting glacier, where glacial streams deposit gravels and sand.

Pangaea—A supercontinent that formed in the Late Paleozoic and held together from 300 to 200 million years ago. Pangaea contained most of the planet's continental land masses.

passive margin—A boundary between continental and oceanic crust that is not a plate boundary, characterized by thick deposits of sedimentary rocks. These margins typically have a flat shallow water shelf, then a steep drop off to deep ocean floor rocks away from the continent.

pediments—Desert surfaces that slope away from the base of a highland and are covered by a thin or discontinuous layer of alluvium and rock fragments.

permafrost—Permanently frozen subsoil that occurs in polar regions and at some high altitudes.

photosynthesis—The process in green plants of trapping solar energy and using it to drive a series of chemical reactions that result in the production of carbohydrates such as glucose or sugar.

plate tectonics—A model that describes the process related to the slow motions of more than a dozen rigid plates of solid rock on the surface of Earth. The plates ride on a deeper layer of partially molten material that is found at depths starting at 60–200 miles (100–320 km) beneath the surface of the continents, and 1–100 miles (1–160 km) beneath the oceans.

playa—Dry lake bed in desert environment.

Precambrian—The oldest broad-grouping of geological time, stretching from the formation of Earth at 4.5 billion years ago and including the Archaean and Proterozoic eons, ending at 540 million years ago.

radiation—Energy in the form of waves.

radiative forcing—The net change in downward minus the upward irradiance at the tropopause, caused by a change in an external driver such as a change in greenhouse gas concentration.

rain shadow—The area on the leeward side of a mountain where the air is descending as a dry air mass, causing little rain to fall.

reef—Wave-resistant framework-supported carbonate or organic mounds generally built by carbonate-secreting organisms. In some usages the term may be used for any shallow ridge of rock lying near the surface of the water.

regolith—The outer surface layer of Earth, consisting of a mixture of soil, organic material, and partially weathered bedrock.

regression—Retreat of the sea from the shoreline, caused by eustatic sea level fall or local effects.

Rossby Waves—Dips and bends in the jet stream path.

saltation—Movement of sand or particles in a series of small jumps and bounces by wind or currents.

seafloor spreading—The process of producing new oceanic crust as volcanic basalt pours out of the depths of Earth, filling the gaps generated by diverging plates. Beneath the mid-oceanic ridges, magma rises from depth in the mantle and forms chambers filled with magma just below the crest of the ridges. The magma in these chambers erupts out through cracks in the roof of the chambers and forms extensive lava flows on the surface. As the two different plates on either side of the magma chamber move apart, these lava flows continuously fill in the gap between the diverging plates, creating new oceanic crust.

sea ice—Ice that has broken off an ice cap or polar sea ice, or calved off a glacier and is floating in open water.

sea level rise—The gradual increase in average height of the mean water mark with respect to the land.

seasons—Variations in the average weather at different times of the year.

Snowball Earth—A time in Earth history when nearly all the water in the planet is frozen, and glaciers exist at low latitudes.

storm surge—A mound of water that moves ahead of and with tropical cyclones and hurricanes, formed by the low pressure in the center of the storm and winds in front of the storm.

stratosphere—Region of the atmosphere above the troposphere that continues to a height of about 31 miles (50 km).

subsidence—The sinking of one surface, such as the land, relative to another surface, such as sea level.

supercontinent cycle—The semi-regular grouping of the planet's landmasses into a single or several large continents that remain stable for a long period of time, then disperse, and eventually come back together as new amalgamated landmasses with a different distribution.

talus—The entire body of rock waste sloping away from the mountains is known as talus, and the sediment composing it is known as sliderock. This rock debris accumulates at the bases of mountain slopes, deposited there by rock falls, slides, and other downslope movements.

thermohaline circulation—Ocean currents that are driven by differences in temperature and salinity of ocean waters.

thermosphere—Region of the atmosphere above the mesosphere that thins upward and extends to about 311 miles (500 km) above the surface.

tides—The periodic rise and fall of the ocean surface, and alternate submersion and exposure of the intertidal zone along coasts.

tidewater glaciers—Glaciers that are partly floating on the ocean, often in steep walled fiords.

till—Glacial drift that was deposited directly by the ice.

tilt—An astronomical measure of how much Earth's rotational axis is inclined relative to the perpendicular to the plane of orbit.

transform boundaries—Places where two plates slide past each other, such as along the San Andreas fault in California, and often have large earthquakes.

transgression—Advance of the sea on the shore, caused by either a eustatic sea level rise or local effects.

troposphere—The lower 36,000 feet (11 km) of the atmosphere.

urban heat island—An effect where cities tend to hold heat more than the countryside.

windward—The side of a mountain facing the oncoming prevailing winds, typically the wet side of a mountain range.

wobble—An astronomical measure of the rotation axis that describes a motion much like a top rapidly spinning and rotating with a wobbling motion, such that the direction of tilt toward or away from the Sun changes, even though the tilt amount stays the same. This wobbling phenomenon is known as precession of the equinoxes.

yardangs—Elongate streamlined wind-eroded ridges, which resemble an overturned ship's hull sticking out of the water.

Further Reading
and Web Sites

BOOKS

Abrahams, A. D., and A. J. Parsons. *Geomorphology of Desert Environments.* Norwell, Mass.: Kluwer Academic Publishers for Chapman and Hall, 1994. This is a comprehensive textbook describing the wide range of landforms and processes in desert environments.

Ahrens, C. D. *Meteorology Today, An Introduction to Weather, Climate, and the Environment.* 6th ed. Pacific Grove, Calif.: Brooks/Cole, 2000. An introductory text for freshman college level on meteorology, weather, and climate.

Ashworth, William, and Charles E. Little. *Encyclopedia of Environmental Studies, New Edition.* New York: Facts On File, 2001. A comprehensive encyclopedia for high-school students covering diverse aspects of the environment.

Bagnold, R. A. *The Physics of Blown Sand and Desert Dunes.* London: Methuen, 1941. This is a classic textbook written based on observations of windblown sand during the war, and was the first to complete a comprehensive study of the physics of windblown sand.

Blackwell, Major James. *Thunder in the Desert, The Strategy and Tactics of the Persian Gulf War.* New York: Bantam, 1991. This is a readable novel-style book that describes the events of the Allied forces in the first Gulf war, including the events that led to the mobility of the sand sheets around Kuwait City.

Botkin, D., and E. Keller. *Environmental Science.* Hoboken, N.J.: John Wiley and Sons, 2003. This is an introductory college-level book that discusses many issues of environmental science.

Bryant, E. A. *Natural Hazards.* Cambridge: Cambridge University Press, 1991. This is a moderately advanced textbook on the science of natural hazards.

Bryson, R., and T. Murray. *Climates of Hunger.* Canberra, Australia: Australian National University Press, 1977. This book describes how drought leads to famine and starvation, with emphasis on the Sahel.

Culliton, Thomas J., Maureen A. Warren, Timothy R. Goodspeed, Davida G. Remer, Carol M. Blackwell, and John McDonough III. *Fifty Years of Population Growth Along the Nation's Coasts, 1960–2010.* Rockville, Md.: National Oceanic and Atmospheric Administration, 1990. This government report shows how half of the nation's population now lives within 60 miles (100 km) of the coast.

Dawson, A. G. *Ice Age Earth.* London: Routledge, 1992. This book describes environmental and geological conditions on the Pleistocene Earth during the ice ages.

Douglas, B., M. Kearney, and S. Leatherman. *Sea Level Rise: History and Consequence.* San Diego, Calif.: Academic Press, International Geophysics Series, vol. 75, 2000. A book describing past and present sea level rise, its causes, and what effects it has on coastal environments.

El-Baz, F., T. M. Kusky, I. Himida, and S. Abdel-Mogheeth, eds. *Ground Water Potential of the Sinai Peninsula, Egypt.* Cairo: Desert Research Center, 1998. This book describes the geology, geomorphology, and groundwater potential in the Sinai Desert of Egypt.

El-Baz, F., and M. Sarawi, eds. *Atlas of the State of Kuwait from Satellite Images.* Ostfildern, Germany: Cantz Publishers, for Kuwait Foundation for the Advancement of Science, 2000. This is a beautifully illustrated atlas of Kuwait, showing the environment before and after the first Gulf war.

Erickson, Jon. *Glacial Geology: How Ice Shapes the Land.* New York: Facts On File, 1996. A book for high-school students about glaciers and their effect on shaping landscapes in glaciated regions.

Intergovernmental Panel on Climate Change 2007. *Climate Change 2007: The Physical Science Basis. Contributions of Working Group I to the Fourth Assessment Report of the Intergovernmental Panel on Climate Change* (Solomon, S., D. Qin, M. Manning, Z. Chen, M. Marquis, K. B. Averyt, M. Tignor, and H. L. Miller, eds.). Cambridge: Cambridge University Press, 2007. This is the most comprehensive and up-to-date scientific assessment of past, present, and future climate change.

Intergovernmental Panel on Climate Change 2007. *Climate Change 2007: Impacts, Adaptation, and Vulnerability. Contributions of Working Group II to the Fourth Assessment Report of the Intergovernmental Panel on Climate Change* (Parry, M., O. Canziani, J. Palutikof, P. van der Linden, and C. Hanson, eds.). Cambridge: Cambridge University Press, 2007. This is the most comprehensive and up-to-date scientific assessment of the impacts of climate change, the vulnerability of natural and human environments, and the potential for response through adaptation.

Intergovernmental Panel on Climate Change 2007. *Climate Change 2007: Mitigation. Contributions of Working Group III to the Fourth Assessment Report of the Intergovernmental Panel on Climate Change* (Metz,

B., O. R. Davidson, P. R. Bosch, R. Dave, and L. A. Meyer, eds.). Cambridge: Cambridge University Press, 2007. This is the most comprehensive and up-to-date assessment of mitigation of future climate change.

Kusky, T. M. *Encyclopedia of Earth Science.* New York: Facts On File, 2004. A comprehensive encyclopedia of earth sciences written for college and high-school audiences and the general public.

Reisner, M. *Cadillac Desert, The American West and Its Disappearing Water.* New York: Penguin, 1986. This is a fascinating book about the history of the development of the west and how critical water resources were to the founding of cities such as Los Angeles.

Starr, J. R., and D. C. Stoll, eds. *The Politics of Scarcity, Water in the Middle East.* Boulder, Colo.: Westview Press, 1988. This book describes the political issues surrounding the severe lack of water with a growing population in the Middle East.

Walker, A. S. *Deserts: Geology and Resources.* U.S. Geological Survey, Publication 421–577, 1996. This government publication covers the geological landforms and characteristics of desert environments.

JOURNAL ARTICLES

Alley, R. B., and M. L. Bender. "Greenland Ice Cores: Frozen in Time." *Scientific American,* February 1998. An article describing the science of taking and analyzing ice cores for climate studies from Greenland.

Crombie, M. K., R. Arvidson, N. C. Sturchio, Z. El-Alfy, and K. Abu Zeid. "Age and isotopic constraints on Pleistocene pluvial episodes in the Western Desert, Egypt." *Paleogeography, Paleoclimatology, Paleoecology* 130 (1997) 337–355. This article presents an analysis of how old the groundwater is in the Western Desert of Egypt and across the Sahara.

Kasting, James F. "Earth's Early Atmosphere." *Science* 259 (1993) 920–925. An assessment of what the earliest atmosphere on Earth was made of and how it evolved into the present atmosphere.

Kunzig, Robert. "Drying of the West." *National Geographic Magazine* 213, no. 2 (2008) 90–113. This article describes the growing drought conditions in the desert Southwest and along the Colorado River.

Kusky, T. M., and F. El Baz. "Structural and tectonic evolution of the Sinai Peninsula, using Landsat data: implications for ground water exploration." *Egyptian Journal of Remote Sensing* 1 (1999) 69–100. This article describes evidence for an ancient wet climate in northern Africa and Sinai.

McKee, E. D., ed. "A study of global sand seas." *U.S. Geological Survey Professional Paper 1052* (1979). A comprehensive description of the different giant sand dune fields, or sand seas, across the world.

Muhs, Daniel R., and James R. Budahan. "Geochemical evidence for the origin of Late Quaternary loess in Central Alaska." *Canadian Journal of Earth Sciences* 43 (2006) 323–337. This paper describes the age and origin of the sand dunes and loess fields of central Alaska.

Pan, Z., M. Segal, and C. Graves. "On the potential change in surface water vapor deposition over the continental United States due to increases in atmospheric greenhouse gases." *Journal of Climate* 19 (2006) 1,576–1,585. This article describes the formation of the global warming hole over the central United States.

Pan, Z., R. W. Arritt, E. S. Takle, W. J. Gutowski Jr., C. J. Anderson, and M. Segal. "Altered hydrologic feedback in a warming climate introduces a 'warming hole.'" *Geophysical Research Letters* 31 (2004). This technical paper describes the physics of forming global warming holes and was the first to describe the atmospheric warming hole that causes the midwestern United States to become wetter and slightly cooler while the rest of the planet gets warmer during global warming.

Schroeder, Peter, Robert Smith, and Kevin Apps. "Solar evolution and the distant future of Earth." *Astronomy and Geophysics* 42, no. 6 (December 2001): 6.26–6.29. This article describes the future of the Sun and Earth.

Webster, D. "Alashan, China's unknown Gobi." *National Geographic* 201, no. 1 (January 2002): 48–75. This well-illustrated article describes the drought and history of parts of the Gobi Desert of China and Mongolia.

WEB SITES

In the past few years numerous Web sites with information about climate change have appeared. Most of these Web sites are free and include historical information about specific causes, hazards, and disasters, real-time monitoring of climate change hotspots around the world, and educational material. The sites listed below have interesting information, statistics, and graphics about these hazards. This book may serve as a useful companion while surfing through the information on the Internet when encountering unfamiliar phrases, terms, or concepts that are not fully explained on the Web site. The following list of Web sites is recommended to help enrich the content of this book and make your exploration of climate change more enjoyable. From these Web sites you will also be able to link to a large variety of climate hazard–related sites. Every effort has been made to ensure the accuracy of the information provided for these Web sites. However, due to the dynamic nature of the Internet, changes might occur, and any inconvenience is regretted.

Federal Emergency Management Agency. FEMA is the nation's premier agency that deals with emergency management and preparation and issues warnings and evacuation orders when disasters appear imminent.

FEMA maintains a Web site that is updated at least daily and includes information of hurricanes, floods, fires, and national flood insurance, and on disaster prevention, preparation, and emergency management. Divided into national and regional sites. Also contains information on costs of disasters, maps, and directions on how to do business with FEMA. Available online. URL: http://www.fema.gov. Accessed January 30, 2008.

Intergovernmental Panel on Climate Change. The IPCC is a scientific intergovernmental body set up by the World Meteorological Organization (WMO) and by the United Nations Environment Program (UNEP). The IPCC is open to all member countries of WMO and UNEP. Governments participate in plenary sessions of the IPCC where main decisions about the IPCC work program are taken and reports are accepted, adopted, and approved. They also participate in the review of IPCC Reports. The IPCC includes hundreds of scientists from all over the world who contribute to the work of the IPCC as authors, contributors, and reviewers. As a United Nations body, the IPCC work aims at the promotion of the United Nations human development goals. The IPCC was established to provide the decision-makers and others interested in climate change with an objective source of information about climate change. The IPCC does not conduct any research nor does it monitor climate-related data or parameters. Its role is to assess on a comprehensive, objective, open, and transparent basis the latest scientific, technical, and socio-economic literature produced worldwide relevant to the understanding of the risk of human-induced climate change, its observed and projected impacts, and options for adaptation and mitigation. IPCC reports should be neutral with respect to policy, although they need to deal objectively with policy relevant to scientific, technical and socio-economic factors. They should be of high scientific and technical standards and aim to reflect a range of views, expertise, and wide geographical coverage. Available online. URL: http://www.ipcc.ch/index.htm. Accessed January 30, 2008.

National Aeronautic and Space Administration (NASA). NASA's Web site on Natural Hazards: Earth scientists around the world use NASA satellite imagery to better understand the causes and effects of natural hazards including climate change. This site posts many public domain images to help people visualize where and when natural hazards occur and to help mitigate their effects. All images in this section are freely available to the public for re-use or re-publication. Available online. URL: http://earthobservatory.nasa.gov/NaturalHazards/. Accessed January 30, 2008.

National Oceanographic and Atmospheric Administration, Hazards Research. Web site about hazards, including climate change. NOAA conducts research and gathers data about the global oceans, atmosphere, space, and Sun, and applies this knowledge to science and service that touch lives of all Americans. NOAA's mission is to describe and predict changes in Earth's environment and conserve and wisely manage the nation's coastal and marine resources. NOAA's strategy consists of seven interrelated strategic goals for environmental assessment, prediction and stewardship. These include 1) advance short-term warnings and forecast services, 2) implement season to interannual climate forecasts, 3) assess and predict decadal to centennial change, 4) promote safe navigation, 5) build sustainable fisheries, 6) recover protected species, and 7) sustain healthy coastal ecosystems. NOAA runs a Web site that includes links to current satellite images of weather hazards, issues warnings of current coastal hazards and disasters, and has an extensive historical and educational service. Available online. URL: http://ngdc.noaa.gov/seg/hazard/tsu.html. Accessed January 30, 2008.

National Weather Service. The National Weather Service, FEMA, and the Red Cross maintain a Web site dedicated to describing how to prepare for severe weather, describing hazards of various types, and providing in depth descriptions of warnings and types of home emergency kits that families should keep in their homes. Available online. URL: http://www.nws.noaa.gov/om/brochures/ffbro.htm. Accessed January 30, 2008.

Natural Hazards Observer. This Web site is the online version of *The Natural Hazards Observer*, the bimonthly periodical of the Natural Hazards Center. It covers current disaster issues; new international, national, and local disaster management, mitigation, and education programs; hazards research; political and policy developments; new information sources and Web sites; upcoming conferences; and recent publications. Distributed to more than 15,000 subscribers in the United States and abroad via their Web site, the Observer focuses on news regarding human adaptation and response to natural hazards and other catastrophic events and provides a forum for concerned individuals to express opinions and generate new ideas through invited personal articles. Available online: URL: http://www.colorado.edu/hazards/o/. Accessed January 30, 2008.

United States Geological Survey, Water Resources. The United States Geological Survey monitors weather and stream flow conditions nationwide and also monitors groundwater levels. Its Web site also contains information on water quality and water use and contains maps and charts of water use–related issues. The Web site has connections to other related Web sites. Available online. URL: http://water.usgs.gov/. Accessed January 30, 2008.

Index

Note: Page numbers in *italic* refer to illustrations, *m* indicates a map, *t* indicates a table.